The American Health System in Perspective

George O. Obikoya

Table of Content

Executive Summary   3

Introduction   6

Rethinking Access to Healthcare in America   9

Healthcare in the US and the Competition/Collaboration Conundrum   46

Healthcare Costs in the US Revisited   82

Does America Need Another Health Sector Reform?   120

Conclusion   154

Executive Summary

The American health system is in flux. Health spending is soaring, over 15%

of the country's gross domestic product (GDP,) and increasing. Its scorecard seems not to reflect this increasing expenditure. Some economists would argue that the country could actually spend increasing amounts of money on health so long as it reduces the costs of healthcare delivery, which would in turn eventually reduce spending. However, studies indicate that American citizens are not necessarily healthier than those of other countries are that spend comparatively less on health. What then is the rationale for this increasing health spending, many would ask. Does the country need to overhaul its health system? That healthcare is playing a relatively minor role in contemporary politicking does not diminish the concern of the ordinary American about the adverse effects of increasing healthcare costs on the wallet, on the one hand and of the potential and more pervasive effects of what some would consider the alarming discrepancy between health spending and healthcare costs on the other. These considerations regardless, to hold that it does not make at least intuitive sense for the strategic intent of the country's health system to be to deliver qualitative health services efficiently, simultaneously reducing healthcare costs, the dual healthcare delivery objectives to which all health systems should in fact aspire, would be most probably tenuous.

Furthermore, that the idea of health sector reform has not gained national prominence since the early nineties is instructive, perhaps of a collective perplexity of the seeming cacophony of often elegant but apparently ineffectual ideas that have characterized attempts in different quarters to fix the health system lately. Yet, we confront potential and real threats to the overall well-being of many in the country on an ongoing basis, Hurricane Katrina, and H5N1 avian influenza sobering, latent festering loci of focused action on the issues on which we were lacking, and of which action one might ask what we should await to propel. Should Americans have to pay increasingly more out-of-pocket health expenses for healthcare to feature on the national political and policy agenda? The endless debates on healthcare cost-sharing formulae highlight the nuance of healthcare delivery issues that should force a reorientation regarding current perceptions of the health system, the essential ingredient of health sector reform more apposite to the inevitable pattern of the evolution of healthcare delivery in the country. The question therefore is not whether the country needs another health sector reform, but the probable consequences of a coalescing conglomerate of disparate forces, agents, and principals alike, whose maneuverings are often antithetical, for a variety of reasons, the noble objectives nonetheless thwarted, left to persist. It becomes therefore moot that health sector is sine qua non to the achievement of the dual healthcare delivery objectives conducted without due cognizance of the peculiarities of its re-conceptualization in its entirety. It is for example an essential ingredient of any health sector reform to attempt to eliminate inequities in access to health services, which yet we could scarcely have achieved, ignoring for say, racial disparities in such access, those regarding a particular race that might not be to the degree of those of some more prominent others.

This e-book examines in-depth the American health system from these

perspectives, in an effort to illuminate the potential issues germane to an all-inclusive reformation attuned to the requirements of contemporary health systems emerging into and blending with the evolutionary forces that would shape future healthcare delivery in the country whose atavistic tendencies are already self-evident. We would therefore embark on this dialectic, our scaling multidirectional, in keeping with the core of the reinvention process that the country's health system crucially needs, a certain flexibility that spawns and nurtures creativity, which in turn engenders quality, the perpetual pursuit of which the various issues and processes revealed would dictate in tandem with the solutions that also emerge.

Introduction

It is arguable that there is consensus that the American health system has

challenges that seem overwhelming and require urgent attention. With the healthcare consumer paying more for healthcare, high numbers of the uninsured, and disparities in access to health services, among others, it is scarcely debatable this consensus among healthcare consumers. Nor is it among policy makers, the potential impact on the different domains of the economy of the soaring health spending the benefits derivable from which in reducing healthcare costs unseen. On the other hand, is it the private sector that would be content about the increasing costs of health and retirement benefits crippling their competitiveness and in effect survival, or would insist for whatever reason that all is well with the country's health system? Could we therefore be wrong to ask if that health system needs or does not need reforming? It is clear what goals health sector reforms aim for in many instances, broad ones at least. Elimination of inequities in access to care, the delivery of qualitative health services to all, and so on would also be health-sector reform objectives relevant to the U.S. However, it is just as clear that achieving these objectives would follow disparate paths in different countries based on the peculiarities of each, for examples regarding demography, geography, even the institutional base available that would be the pillars literally of some of these healthcare reform efforts. Thus, should we not consider these factors in our examination of the American health system with a view to ensuring that we determine specific reform goals, and the means to achieving them?

The achievement of specific reform goals requires a thorough appraisal of the

health system, which is the essential thrust of this e-book. The premise for this thrust is the necessity for such understanding being a determined effort to re-conceptualize health sector reform in keeping with the perennial changes in healthcare delivery models, the technologies that fuel so to say the motorization of the transactions involved in the healthcare delivery process crucial to its survival let alone progress. We would explore in this e-book some of the salient issues and processes whose operations are crucial to this motorization, which drives the core of healthcare delivery with a view to appreciating their effectiveness and efficiency in achieving the dual healthcare delivery objectives that the health system should appropriately pursue and with vigor. This is more so that it is clearly unsustainable for the country to continue to spend increasing percentages of its gross domestic product (GDP) on healthcare, considering in fact that it would need to spend even more were such a determined effort at curtailing health spending, not vigorously pursued, along with and without prejudice to the delivery of qualitative healthcare. It is also the case that with the increasing emphasis on the focus of healthcare being on the consumer, that satisfaction with the country's healthcare would depend not just on the quality of the services received, but on the ability of the healthcare consumer to receive these services at much less costs. The basic tenets of the dual healthcare delivery objectives apply therefore to at all levels, of the healthcare stakeholder spectrum.

There is no doubt therefore about the need for such efforts as ours to decompose the health system to enable the in-depth understanding of the issues and processes that underlie healthcare delivery in the country, and that perhaps hinder its effectiveness, hence in the process determine the most appropriate solutions to the problems.

Rethinking Access To Healthcare in America

Scientists at the University of Michigan led by Dr. Robert Axelrod recently

published a paper in the September 5, 2006 issue of the *Proceedings of the National Academy of Sciences*, inspired by the "game theory", in which they hypothesized about all cancer cells not being equally endowed and requiring collaboration with other cells to become established full-blown cancer. As already established cancer cells interact with normal stromal cells, which latter support and facilitate tumor growth, hence adjoining pre-cancerous cells could possibly collaborate to protect one another, according to the researchers. Thus, the effect of collaborating could be bidirectional, contiguous cells could provide scarce resources, such as some forms of growth factors needed by other cells to aid the mutations required for the emergence of the genetic structure of a cancer cell, on the one hand, or protect one another, on the other. Could manipulating the genetic constituents of cells help prevent the negative, and reinforce the positive, results of cellular collaboration? Incidentally, a study published in the October 06, 2006 issue of *Science* noted that experiments on a "fairness" game pointed toward the right dorsolateral prefrontal cortex (DLPFC) of the brain helps individuals suppress selfish urges in clearly unfair situations, even at their own expense[2], the suppression lifted upon using a mild electric current to momentarily immobilize the DLPFC. During the experiment, individuals with disabled right-side dorsolateral prefrontal cortexes snatched how much money they could from obviously uneven transactions, knowing it to be so, clearly unable to help themselves. The Swiss/American team that conducted the research noted that, despite the conflicts, wars, and crimes, which characterize human society, human beings are inherently cooperative, and are in fact unique among species in exhibiting "reciprocal fairness," able to punish others for unfair behavior, even if it hurt those doing the punishing. This, according to lead researcher Ernst Fehr, director of the Institute for Empirical Research in Economics at the University of Zurich is because, we are highly evolved socially, punishing unfairness helping to "sustain cooperation in groups." This in turn provides competitive edge, which no doubt has been crucial to the evolutionary success of humankind. Fehr further noted, "The big surprise is that a relatively minor inhibition of the right DLPFC removes or weakens the subject's ability to override their self-interest." The experiment indicates that the right DLPFC is central to our social behavior, helping us resist the powerful urges for sex, money, and avarice associated with more primitive brain areas outside the cortex, although it is unclear if it functions alike in all of us, including psychopaths and criminals. The researchers are looking into this, and into the role of the seemingly more mysterious left DLPFC. There might in fact be genetic involvement in the extent to which these cortical areas perform their functions in different persons, perhaps in some, not even at all, but suffice to say that in general, most human beings are inclined to collaborate. This attribute would feature prominently in our discussion here on the various issues pertinent to improving access to health care. There is indeed, ample evidence the genes play an important role in many aspects of our lives, including in diseases, for examples, psychiatric and behavioral disorders, such as bipolar disorders and anxiety[3, 4], Biederman and associates[3] noting that over 25%

10

of first-degree relatives of children that had ADHD also did, versus 5% of controls without the condition. Our increasing knowledge of the genetic basis of disease is profoundly changing healthcare delivery, the growing integration of biotechnology and personalized healthcare, especially customizing medications based on genetic information, an area where American scientists are at the forefront of cutting-edge research. It is also one, which would have, among others that we would discuss here, equally far-reaching implications for our conceptualization of and access to care in the country, and indeed, in many others, in the years ahead. A recent New York Times report, for example, noted that the demand for novel cancer treatments continues although access to some is falling as prices increasess. Indeed, the paper noted that the "rise in cancer drug prices is a pointer to broader trends increasing health care costs in the country, costs that seem to have little impact on demand, with patients facing harsh prognoses frantic for new, more effective medications, insurers essentially powerless to negotiate prices or disallow coverage. Besides, the difficulty replacing most cancer medications with another, which does not exactly foster competition amongst pharmaceutical firms, the public resists attempts by insurers to promote the use of generics rather than new cancer medications, and the law prohibits Medicare factoring costs into treatment coverage. Furthermore, the Food and Drug Administration (FDA) does not regulate medications' prices as part of its review procedure. For these are some of the reasons, among others, the prices of cancer medications keep rising, in fact faster than overall health care inflation. Indeed, estimates of worldwide spending on the medications showed, between 2004 and 2009 an increase more than twice over to $55 billions, the increasing costs of these medications, reducing access to them, which the defect in public policy to rein in soaring prices could only aggravate. With many patients' co-payments for their cancer medications as much as 20%, which could be financially crippling for many with one, let alone, multiple medications, access to these drugs is a major healthcare delivery issue. Indeed, an issue warrants urgent attention as part of efforts to make healthcare more accessible in the country, it therefore also raises some important questions. That the country's scientists swept the 2006 Nobel Prizes in the sciences, five Americans winning in the medicine, physics and chemistry categories, is no doubt, testimony to academic/training excellence. However, it also reflects the country's lavish funding of research, $301.5 billion in 2004 alone, for example, on research and development in industry and universities, according to the U.S National Science Foundation, over what the U.K., Canada, France, Germany, Italy, and Japan combined, did in the same years. In fact, the relationship between excellence and research funding seems to be in the main, direct. It is noteworthy also that some of these Nobel laureates have made significant discoveries with potentially profound implications for our understanding of and treatment of diseases. Roger Kornberg, a professor at the Stanford University School of Medicine in California, won this year's Chemistry prize, according to the citation of the Royal Swedish Academy of Sciences for "his fundamental studies concerning how the information stored in the genes is copied, and then transferred to those parts of the cells that produce proteins". His work opens new opportunities for our understanding of the transcription process, which is crucial for stem cells to transform into different kinds of specific cells. It also creates prospects for growing transplant tissue in the lab someday, and as many diseases for examples cancers and heart diseases result from dysfunctional transcription, for the more effective treatment of these and other diseases. The works of Stanford Professor Andrew Fire and colleague Craig Mello of the University of Massachusetts, who share the Nobel Prize in Medicine on ribonucleic acid interference (RNAi), how RNA could turn off genes, including those that are aberrant and disease-forming, would certainly revolutionize how we treat many diseases, including cancers and AIDS. It is therefore, reasonable to suggest that the U.S., and indeed, other countries, should not only support, but step-up support for research. However, with the new drugs that these researches spawn too costly for most people to access would some not query the wisdom in spending taxpayers' money on the researches, or at least wonder if there was no way we could make the drugs more accessible to patients? Indeed, Senate leaders in late September 2006 introduced a bill that would authorize, over a five-year period, $20 billion in new spending to support science and math education and broaden federal research programs[6]. The NIH's National Institute of General Medical Sciences (NIGMS) started to support the work of Fire in 1987 and Mello in 1999, and has over the years, provided them almost $8.5 million[7]. The NIH's National Institute of Child Health and Human Development also provided over $3 million to support Dr. Mello's researches, these supports, evidence of the significance of both supporting new investigators and keeping investigator-initiated ideas afloat. The Nobelists, according to NIH Director Elias A. Zerhouni, M.D. "...used experiments with nematode worms to find a mechanism that can silence genes in humans. Many diseases develop when genes don't work properly, so RNA interference offers a tremendous potential to create a new generation of drugs targeted to these and other conditions." "This honor underscores the fundamental role that basic research plays in advancing our understanding of health", Jeremy M. Berg, Ph.D., NIGMS director, also observed. Yet, as noted earlier, the new generation of drugs that these basic researchers carried over into other basic and applied researches spawn, are hardly accessible to the people that funded the basic researches in the first place. Should it be surprising then that some would ask why a fundamental reappraisal of the admittedly complex interrelationships between R&D funding and the utilization of its outcomes, particularly in the applied health and pharmaceutical industries should not just be legitimate, but urgent, if we were indeed, serious about tackling the issues around which improving accessibility to care hinge? Should we not indeed, be seeking ways to strengthen the positive elements of these multifarious, intersectoral, collaborative efforts and eliminating their negative elements? Is this not even more so considering that research indicates that R&D in fact also contributes to economic growth and development, an added incentive for countries to keep funding these research efforts?

The U.S. Bureau of Economic Analysis (BEA) estimates utilizing data from the

National Science Foundation's (NSF) annual surveys of government, academic, industry, and non-profit R&D expenditures indicate that research and development (R&D) accounted for a considerable portion of the resurgence in U.S. economic growth in recent years, contributing 6.5% to economic growth between 1995 and 2002s. Incidentally, as BEA Director Steve Landefeld noted, almost 40% of the country's productivity and growth is unaccounted for in the gross domestic product (GDP), due mainly to unavailability of dependable data in some economic sectors. Indeed, NSF and agencies in many other countries gather far-reaching R&D expenditure data as R&D is critical to economic growth and social welfare, its benefits, sometimes far beyond expectations, the resources organizations allocate to R&D, very much influencing not only economic growth but also the country's competitiveness on the global stage. There is no doubt about considering R&D as an investment or asset rather than an expense, since the return on such investments often do not materialize until many years later and often do as marketable and indeed, often profitable, products/services. Including R&D in the GDP as an investment noted BEA would result in business investment being $178 billion higher than otherwise. Coupled with the beneficial effects of R&D on the economy is also that of health, whose benefits in part derive direct from investments in R&D, as we have noted earlier, and whose decline, therefore, suggests, potential adverse consequences for economic growth and sustainable development. It is intuitive therefore, to ensure continued investments in R&D, just as it is to ensure that the citizenry enjoys the benefits of such investments, in terms of their health and social welfare, among others, for the effects of the investments on the economy to manifest. In other words, we have to start looking at access to health in more-fundamental ways, exploring the many pertinent issues involved, including some of the more subterranean, even if we had to ferret out the answers we need. This is more considering the significance of access to healthcare to the achievement of the dual healthcare delivery goals of providing qualitative health services, simultaneously reducing health spending, goals that the American heath system, or any health system worldwide, for that matter, would have to start to pursue vigorously sooner than later. In view of the increasingly limited resources available for healthcare delivery in many countries, and the correspondingly increasing expectations of the public of health services, a change in orientation toward achieving the dual healthcare delivery goals, is to say the least, an appropriate response to major contemporary healthcare delivery challenges. Some consider the U.S. economy is slowing down, despite that, the federal budget deficit estimate for the fiscal year just completed has fallen to $250 billion, the economy's tax revenues, mostly from corporate profits, the chief reason. The most recent estimates of the Congressional Budget Office (CBO) are $10 billion less than its August 2006 estimates, and even much less than White House's July 2006 $296 billion estimates, not to mention the $318 billion and $413 billion deficits, posted in 2005, and 2004, respectively. Some are holding their breath, literally, expecting the deficit to be worse next year. However, with unemployment falling 4.6% in September 2006 and the Dow Jones industrial average attaining record highs in early October, coupled with the deficit weighed against the size of the U.S. economy, the comparison economists deem most crucial, the deficit thus even more remarkable, many would argue that the economy is faring well. With the deficit this year 1.9% GDP, versus 6% in 1983, for example, this conclusion seems warranted, although the imminent retirement of baby-boomers, an increasingly aging population, and an increasingly diverse population with equally varied disease patterns, among several other factors that would increase spending on

Social Security and Medicare, could potentially worsen the deficits in the long term. Income taxes and payroll taxes for Social Security, Medicare and unemployment insurance increased by just 7%, why some contend that lower- and middle-income people benefit much less from the current economic recovery. In comparison for example, corporate profits' taxes, and from the rich, and small businesses, increased by 27% relative to last year, non-withheld tax receipts, by 19%. There are two diametrically opposed issues stemming from these considerations, regarding access to healthcare, first, the potential worsening of the deficits due to increasing health spending the factors mentioned above could engender further compromising access to healthcare as health insurance becomes even less affordable to many. Second, potential increase in tax-revenue generation could further depreciate the ability of many to afford health insurance, hence to access care. The two issues, with additional consequences that have potentially-serious implications for access to healthcare, therefore dovetail to create the troubling result that is adversative, in many ways, not just to the achievement of the dual healthcare delivery goals, but indeed, to buoyancy of the overall economy of the country, at large. This again, underscores the need for a more global approach to exploring the issue of access to healthcare in the U.S., for us to be able to decipher the real issues involved, prioritize them, and address them vigorously. This is more so because, even in the short term, these issues could compromise access to healthcare sufficiently for their effects on the health of the populace, and on the economy to be excruciatingly longer lasting, and more difficult to rectify. With soaring health spending already a major cause for concern in the U.S., this problem more widespread globally than might be immediately obvious, the ripple the combination of worsening budget deficit and increasing taxes could generate could be potentially "catastrophic". Consider for example that OECD Health Data 2006 noted that health spending keeps increasing in OECD countries and that the persistence of these trends would mean that governments will have to raise taxes, slash spending in other

16

areas or make their citizens fund more out-of-pocket, to maintain their current healthcare systems[10]. These data indicate that from 1990-2004, health spending increased faster than GDP in every OECD country including the U.S., except Finland, accounting for 7% , 8.8%, and 8.9% of GDP on average across OECD countries in 1990, 2003, and 2004, respectively (figure 1.) In most OECD countries, taxes fund most healthcare costs, 73% of health spending publicly funded in 2004, averagely.

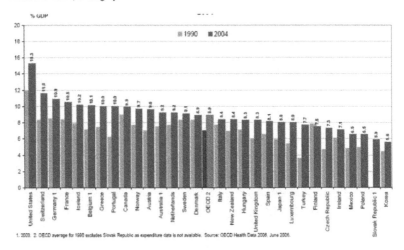

Figure 1: Change in health expenditure as share of GDP in OECD countries (1990&2004)[10]

It is therefore important to governments to have the funds available to fund healthcare delivery at all times. However, how easy this would increasingly be considering the projected increase in health spending as a percentage of GDP, for a variety of reasons such as the aging population in many developed countries, increasing medication costs, and costs of new medical technologies, among

17

others, remains conjectural. Public share of health spending in the U.S has increased in recent times, from 40% to 45% between 1990 and 2004. Although it is still not as much as the contribution of the private sector, which remains dominant, as it spends much more money overall on health than other countries[10], its public spending on health per capita is still higher than that in most other OECD countries. In 2004, this was US$6,100 (adjusted for purchasing power parity), more than twice the OECD average of US$2,550 USD in 2004[11]. Indeed, between 1999 and 2004, U.S health spending per capita hiked in real terms by 5.9% per year on average, more than the 5.2% per annum OECD average. The country is also spending more on pharmaceuticals, 8.5%, and 12.3% of total health spending in 1994 and 2004, respectively, and US$752 per capita on pharmaceuticals in 2004, more than any other country, followed by France. The immediate question remains how the U.S intends to continue to fund these increases in health spending, which are likely to increase even further with baby-boomers retiring in numbers, and the population aging increasingly, among other factors. The next concerns what effects, the "cash crunch" on the U.S. health system would have on access to health services, particularly among the middle-class and lower-income classes. With private health insurance increasingly inaccessible to many in these classes, for a variety of reasons mostly cost-related, direct, out-of-pocket spending also increasing, as one would expect would follow from the former, what would be the additional consequences of these developments coupled with the those of the "cash crunch" mentioned earlier on accessibility to healthcare delivery? Again, these and other crucial issues regarding accessibility to care need urgent attention were we to expect to improve access to care in the country. As noted earlier, we have to start to explore the problem of access to care from its roots to make any meaningful positive changes to it. There is little if any doubt about the complexity of the issues involved but we could solve these problems by adopting simple approaches. One such involves identifying the key issues in our particular jurisdiction relevant to healthcare accessibility, decomposing these issues, in the process exposing the sub-issues and processes, and applying the necessary measures, including deploying the appropriate healthcare information and communication technologies, to tackling them. This approach, which we would term process cycle analysis, would likely reveal the solutions we seek, including the healthcare ICT that could be crucial in many cases to facilitating access to health services by the many that otherwise would have, for a variety of reasons, lacked such access.

Our discussion so far clearly indicates that the issues germane to healthcare accessibility are legion, and diverse, some health, others non-health-related, but all in the end contributing, and indeed, potentially, hindering access to care. This underscores the point we made earlier about the need for collaboration between these different domains for the successful resolution of the problem of access to care. This point is intriguing considering that it leads us inevitably to the competition/collaboration conundrum, a natural dyadic that we have exploited and that has served us well evolutionarily, but which we seem to need to exploit even more in our attempts to solve the problem of accessibility to health services not just in the U.S., but worldwide. Essentially, we need to fine tune the elements of these natural tendencies, making them work for each other, so that for example, in generating tax revenues from corporate organizations, we do not run them aground, which would disrupt the balance of the conundrum at other levels, for example, where the resources for survival, let alone healthcare become scarcer. The consequences of such disruptions could reverberate across spectra, worsening the overall health of the country, further increasing the need for more health spending, simultaneously compromising the economy, creating a cascade down potential added complications regarding the country's healthcare delivery, and even its economy. Private payments for health financed by private insurance have close ties with the employers responsible for the healthcare of millions of Americans, private health insurance, and even where it accounts for only about 6% of total health spending on average across OECD countries, it is important for certain peoples in Germany and the Netherlands. It is even more important in the U.S for most of non-seniors, constituting 37% of health spending in 2004, between 10% and 15% in Canada and France, where it offers optional, additional coverage in these countries' public health systems. Furthermore, private sources tend to be more crucial in funding medications, than for hospital or ambulatory care, as many publicly financed health insurance programs do not cover the former that well, public coverage of spending on drugs in the U.S in 2004, 34%, versus 38% in Canada, 12% in Mexico, over 66% such countries as Sweden, France, and Germany[10]. This again brings to the fore the point made earlier about the need to explore ways to facilitate access to medications in the U.S., in particular the expensive new medications for the treatment of such conditions as cancer, the basic research that often lead to which the public which increasingly funds, yet access to which medications it increasingly lacks. This is the more pertinent considering the increasing private sourcing of funds for medications in the country, which also explains the need to maintain the balance between competition and collaboration mentioned earlier considering the significant roles private employers play in sourcing these funds. In other words, our efforts to ensure ready accessibility to healthcare would involve tweaking the conundrum without tilting the balance. With regard employers for example, in taxing them, or encouraging/coercing them as in Maryland that in January 2006, passed a law requiring firms with 10,000 or more workers in the state, to spend at least 8% of their payrolls on health insurance, or pay the difference into a state Medicaid fund, ensure we do not compromise their very existence. This also means that we do not hinder their ability to compete both within the country, and abroad. With regard, individuals, as with the Massachusetts law in April 2006, mandating all residents to purchase health insurance by July 1, 2007, or face a fine, we are as the state did, careful to expand the choices to include a number of novel and low-priced policies, from about $250 per month to almost free, from private insurers the state subsidizes. This is not to further and paradoxically compromise accessibility to care by fiat, assuming that the state's over half a million uninsured would no longer be able to flock the ER, at taxpayers' expense, part of the very problem once termed "freedom to mooch," the new law aims to solve. We should also ensure that those in the low-income brackets would be able to afford the new, "cheaper", policies, to ensure we are indeed solving the healthcare accessibility problem we set out to solve. Let us illustrate the need for maintaining the competition/collaboration balance in ensuring access to health services with an example from the technical domain. This is in keeping with the point we made earlier about the eclectic nature of the issues pertinent to the problems of healthcare accessibility, and the need to identify them in any particular health jurisdiction to enhance the prospects of finding solutions to the problem. One dimension of access to care from the technical perspective was evident earlier this year with the introduction of the new Medicare Part D prescription drug benefit that had thousands of elderly and disabled Americans, their pharmacists struggling to tackle a number of start-up problems blamed in part on the apparently unanticipated load on the applicable information systems networks. The result was the denial/lack of access to care by the very beneficiaries of the program, in particular poor and infirmed seniors switching from state Medicaid programs to the new Medicare plans, with many states having to intervene, pledging to pay for medications for any low-income senior inadvertently rejected by the systems. Such denial/lack of access to care occasioned by technological flaws also need our attention as part of our overall efforts at ensuring access to care. So does the lack of the appropriate technologies in the first place compromising access to care, and does the sort of major flaws recently reported for a Medicaid and Medicare computer network, which has sensitive financial data on recipients. According to the New York Times article that carried the story on October 08, 2006, it also links the databank of the Centers for Medicare and Medicaid Services to many organizations, for examples, banks, nursing homes, clinics, hospitals, insurance firms, and health plans, among others12. A recent Government Accountability Office (GAO) investigation revealed that the system lacks vital information security controls, strict password controls with passwords too simple and guessable, encryption for the Medicare and Medicaid data, and even comprehensive records on monitoring of the network, including who use it and why, which suggests no way to know if security breaches had already occurred. GAO officials however noted that the flaws makes the system vulnerable to possible unauthorized access to sensitive medical information on recipients, and to a major disruption of services that could potentially compromise access to care by millions of people. As Senator Charles E. Grassley, Republican of Iowa, and chairman of the Finance Committee that oversees Medicare and Medicaid, who called for the investigation noted, Medicare officials ought to "to get on top of these shortcomings immediately." He added, "Beneficiaries not only rely on Medicare for their health care coverage, they expect that the private information they entrust to the government is kept private, safe and secure". Here again, an analytical approach to revealing the issues involved would no doubt facilitate rectifying these problems and move us closer to our goals of ensuring access to care for all. This universal access has nothing to do with the funding system of the health system in question, although in this instance, we refer to one with a mix of public and private funds. In other words, just as we are flexible in defining accessibility to care, conceptualizing it in broad rather than exclusive terms, we should also view universal access to care this way, which would facilitate the sort of decomposition/exposition exercise we termed process cycle analysis, crucial to deciphering and solving healthcare accessibility issues in particular healthcare jurisdictions. Thus, there are individuals in both the U.S and Canada that live in remote locations with little, and albeit difficult access to health services. In a sense, the issues that they face are similar, lack of access to care, and living in remote locations, but not only do they live in different countries, with different health funding systems, the remoteness might be due to geographical terrain in one instance, a clinic just a few kilometers away but sheer distance in another. In both instances, implementing telemedicine would help but there might be cross-territorial credentialing issues still in the way of access to care in one, but not in the other location. The problem might in fact have to do with reimbursement for electronic healthcare delivery in one jurisdiction, the issue not a problem in the other. Each jurisdiction could therefore aim for universal access to care but from different perspectives. These perspectives would in part determine the peculiarities of the technical challenges they would face, and the ways to resolve them. Even with those technical issues that seem to cut across borders, for example, the interoperability of disparate healthcare software and other ICT, each jurisdiction could confront problems unique to it based for example, on the nature and extent of its technical and institutional infrastructures, among others, not to mention in fact, the different meanings even the word connotes. The important thing is that it is difficult if not impossible for information communication and sharing with software that do not in effect "speak" with each other, which may essentially compromise access to care. The Commission on Systemic Interoperability, or CSI, which the U.S Congress and President George W. Bush in the Medicare Modernization Act created published its recommendations on an interoperable system of health information in October 2005, in a report titled "Ending the Document Game: Connecting and Transforming Your Healthcare through Information Technology[13]". Focused on the adoption of healthcare ICT and its connectivity, besides interoperability, the commission noted, among its fourteen specific recommendations, real life case histories of the benefits accruable from the proper application of automation in healthcare delivery, including regarding access to care. Thus, the technical dimension of access to healthcare is just as crucial to explore at the health jurisdiction level, although the issues that might emerge in so doing would transcend that particular jurisdiction, and might indeed, be national in scope. It is no doubt important for different health information systems and software applications to "speak" with one another and to exchange data accurately, efficiently, effectively, and reliably, and in many instances in real time. In terms of patient management, we could effectively have denied access to care, in its broader sense, to a patient, an ER doctor unable to acquire and use critical information, not ensuring the interoperability of disparate information systems. For example, we would have essentially not only denied access to care to that patient but in the process put his/her life in jeopardy, for example, the information systems of the patient's GP, were there any at all, and of the ER department to which he or she lies unable to communicate. Meanwhile, the patient is perhaps even slipping into coma, suspended precariously in the twilight of life.

This example from the technical domain also underscores the benefits of our approach at eliciting required information on the variety of issues involved in solving healthcare access problems. Should it not be part of the package of efforts by the health jurisdiction where the above event occurred or could potentially occur to not only encourage its doctors and other healthcare professionals to acquire and implement the healthcare ICT needed for such doctor/doctor information exchange, but to ensure the interoperability of these disparate systems? Should health jurisdiction not be examining regulation and credentialing issues as important parts of this package as well? Considering the excess morbidity that could result were a doctor not able to contact say a patient via text message that is not reachable otherwise regarding a positive bacterial culture and the need to pick up the required antibiotic at the nearest pharmacy, the prescription made electronically. Would not have not only denied access to care to that patient because the doctor did not send the text message for fear of not receiving reimbursement for the service, and would we not be negating our efforts to achieve the dual healthcare delivery goals in so doing? In other words, would we not have failed to deliver qualitative healthcare, but also ended up increasing health spending taking care of the excess morbidity that our inaction occasioned, if in fact the patient did not end up dying? Thus, we need to broaden our concept of accessibility to care and explore our options in their full ramifications. We should not proceed too far down the road of implementing electronic health records for example, without resolving the problems of interoperability, as pervasive EHR adoption could exacerbate these problems and complicate the development of interoperability standards. Otherwise, we might be creating a situation wherein we invest millions of dollars in healthcare ICT that would not result in our achieving the cross-country data exchange capability we set out to, but also thereby further compromise access to care, and indeed, our ability to achieve the dual healthcare delivery objectives of qualitative health services provision simultaneously reducing health spending. We need to continue to address all the relevant issues both technical and non-technical that could make our quest for sophisticated electronic data and information exchange with health systems able to interpret and integrate functionalities automatically, say lab results or X-rays of clinic A to hospital B. With doctors in either facility able to access these data, information, and images whenever in the course of patient management, we could say then that we have truly achieved comprehensive access to care by patients, the first critical step in the provision of qualitative care, and the reduction in healthcare costs that the efficiency and effectiveness of healthcare delivery engender. Besides the issues we have discussed thus far are many others that need careful exploration to get to the roots of the healthcare accessibility problems a health jurisdiction faces, such as those relating albeit not exclusively to the technical domain mentioned including the privacy and confidentiality, which could also compromise healthcare access. This means examining all sides of any technical issue, conceptualizing these issues in business rather than strictly technical terms, the implications of not addressing the issues and seeking the appropriate solutions to the problems, therefore staring us more squarely in the face, literally, spurring us into action, if we had not started. Such an approach for example would enable us to see more clearly the futility in hoarding data and information, in other words, being stuck in the competitive mode, thereby tipping the competition/collaboration balance unfavorably for what we plan to achieve in healthcare delivery, the dual healthcare delivery goals, healthcare accessibility, its primary component. It is relatively common for example, in the health sector to have 'silos' of data/information systems, even within the same healthcare organization, communication and sharing with colleagues and departments, almost nonexistent, in some cases, the competition often underlying this situation taken way too far for either the individuals' or organization's good. Granted that costs and poor planning might be the cause of the lack of inter-departmental communication, but researchers that deliberately keep the results of their works away from colleagues, no doubt have other motives, most often competitive. This underscores the need to strike the right balance between competition and collaboration in the ever-present interplay mentioned above, achievable via the implementation of the necessary healthcare ICT for data/information communication and sharing in institutions, and the elimination of whatever local-and national-related barriers hindering data/information exchange. To derive maximum benefits from such an exchange, it has to transcend organizational boundaries. In other words, scientists, clinicians, and researchers, among other healthcare data/information users ought to be able to communicate and share information with colleagues and others in other organizations, within and even outside the country. This calls for, and at the same time points to the difficulty in the need to agree on how to transmit data/information among these disparate entities, again highlighting the need for consensus on standards. This would facilitate the integration of the Regional Health Information Networks (RHIN) springing up in the states, for example, into a formidable National Health Information Network (NHIN,) making access to healthcare ever more comprehensive, and efficient. As we have noted thus far, reframing access to healthcare delivery in our minds is a crucial first step in our efforts to improve the quality of healthcare delivery in the country, where according to the U.S. Census Bureau, the number of persons that have no health insurance increased to 45 million in 2003, up by 1.4 million people[14]. Again, we need to examine these figures closely to see the underlying issues involved following the principles enunciated above, namely process cycle analysis, to be able to tackle these issues most effectively. Small and medium sized firms for example employ many of these uninsured Americans. On account of the perception of their denial the capacity to purchase quality health coverage for their employees comparable with the benefits large, multi-state firms, offer their workers, such as employees of 83% of firms with over 5,000 workers able to choose from more than one health plan versus just 10% in firms with less than 50 workers, Congress acted. On June 19, 2003, a bipartisan House passed the Small Business Health Fairness Act (H.R. 660), expected to increase access appreciably to health coverage for uninsured persons and their families countrywide by establishing Association Health Plans (AHPs), a show of the House's obligation to address the issue of access to healthcare. AHPs enable small businesses to collaborate, essentially to band together via associations and buy quality health care for employees/families at reduced costs, buoy their advantage with health care providers, free them expensive state-ordered benefit packages, and reduce overheads by up to 30%, benefits that scale economies already confer on large firms and unions. Their strict eligibility criteria and solvency standards, among others also aimed at guaranteeing workers' interests, ensure workers receive

27

adequate and qualitative coverage, this law, among others, 16 healthcare ICT-related bills in the House/Senate in 2005, another key dimension, the legislative and regulatory, crucial to considerations of healthcare accessibility in the U.S., and in fact in many other countries. Indeed, in this context, regarding the U.S., we should aim to understand the dynamics of the uninsured in America, considering certain generally known facts about this population, which if left unattended to, could render the overall efforts at achieving the dual healthcare delivery goals in the country essentially futile. We should establish for example why most young Americans do not buy health insurance, and many who qualify for Medicaid or for the State Children's Health Insurance Program (SCHIP), the latter established in 1997 to provide coverage to uninsured low-income children unqualified for Medicaid, do not enroll for these programs. We also need to understand fully why many Americans that could afford health insurance do not purchase one, and among many others, the problems associated with the policy of not turning anyone back from American ERs, and so forth, its cost implications, and whether to modify it, and how. We also need to study the results of measures taken by some states such as Maryland mentioned above, compelling everyone to purchase health insurance, to see if they are applicable in other states, in their current or modified forms, or not at all. The dimensions of access to care are indeed, many and complex. This is why we need to incorporate the competition/collaboration balance into our analysis, for example, in tackling the issues relating to moral hazard the unrestricted use of the ER including by the uninsured, illegal immigrants, the poor, and others, spawns. Could there be a triage process for example networked with but antecedent to the ER to curtail abuse of the policy, for example, calling a certain number, or even from a certain location, where a triage nurse could see via video the patient, and conduct a quick interview? Could we not set up the healthcare ICT enabling this triage nurse for example to even take the vital signs, and determine whether, with some initial treatment/counsel, the patient should visit the ER, or his or GP soonest, or neither? Would collaborating with young people rather than competing for the funds they would rather use to dine out or for entertainment, for example, offering them incentives, or even a special package of health insurance not encourage them to purchase some form of health insurance rather than none at all? Could such packages not entail deploying the appropriate technologies, for example, via cellular phone to meet their health needs, for example, based on the tripartite primary, secondary, and tertiary prevention paradigm? Could such programs not ensure their access to health, albeit on their own terms, but still worth the while in their interest and that of society at large, and would such efforts not be contributing overall to the achievement of the dual healthcare delivery objectives?

W e could in fact do much in solving the various problems of access to

healthcare adopting this analytic approach that breaks down the issues and focuses on each one in-depth, decomposing it, its components surfacing in the process as would the solutions to them, including the healthcare ICT-related. There is no doubt about the waste, and the increased morbidities and mortalities that result from the present fragmented state of the country's health systems. The seeming disinterest of the health industry over the years in healthcare ICT has not made matters better, and only in recent years is the evidently increasing momentum spurring the industry into action in this regard. We are starting to see intersectoral collaboration in promoting the widespread diffusion of these technologies, which research evidence indicates have the potential to help us achieve the dual healthcare delivery goals. That bodies such as the American Health Information Community set up by the HHS in late 2005 to provide it counsel on facilitating EHR adoption, have many members from the business sector confirms the new orientation toward multi-faceted collaborative efforts in tackling the equally multidimensional healthcare delivery issues, including those concerning access to care. This again, underscores the need for balance between competition, which among these same business persons/groups would augur well for the implementation and use of novel technologies for example in healthcare delivery, and collaboration among them, which would facilitate the development of standards for interoperability of the disparate technologies they market to the health sector, among others. Both competition and collaboration are no doubt required elements of the efforts toward achieving the dual healthcare delivery goals, striking a balance between them in this regard also doubtless key. The same principles apply to resolving the technical issues in the way of interoperable data/information exchange for example, the professionals that would explore and find the solutions to the relevant technological issues of necessity setting aside their competitive leanings to collaborate in the needed efforts to achieve these goals. They would need to join ongoing and planned initiatives in their jurisdictions to contribute their quota, and undertake process cycle analyses in their respective domains, determining the sub-issues and processes to address and with the technologies, policies, and methodologies required. Efforts to achieve the dual healthcare delivery goals need the involvement of all healthcare stakeholders, which would make the starting point for identifying the issues to decompose even more generic, and create enhanced opportunities to identify the real issues and processes that need modifying, facilitating or excluding, to improve the overall healthcare delivery process, including access to health services. It is still a long way to the employment of teleportation in access to healthcare delivery, but we should not forget in our exploration of this issue to examine the emerging technologies that could help us achieve this goal, which is in keeping with our premise to encourage mindset change in our approach to the issue. Danish physicists for example, recently teleported information from light to matter, the alliance of quantum communication and computing closer to reality, improving on earlier works teleporting similar objects, for example, light or single atoms, over short distances from one spot to the next in seconds[15]. Professor Eugene Polzik and associates at the Niels Bohr Institute at the University of Copenhagen, Denmark have now used both light and matter, which according to him, "... is one step further because, for the first time, it involves teleportation between light and matter, two different objects. One is the carrier of information and the other one is the storage medium." The experiment reported in *Nature*, in October 2006, which for the first time involved a macroscopic atomic object that had thousands of billions of atoms, the information teleported over a distance of half a meter, which the team believes they could still extend, no doubt has the potential to facilitate access between two locations. This technology might some day have applications in healthcare delivery including in improving access to care, for example by individuals in remote locations to scarce experts beamed to where they are. Noted Polzik "Our method allows teleportation to be taken over longer distances because it involves light as the carrier of entanglement", quantum entanglement involving interweaving two or more particles without physical contact. The refinement of this technique might make such "beaming" of experts or even patients to healthcare facilities to receive care, perhaps, critical, that they need, happen sooner than we imagine. In any case, what Polzik's team achieved, again emphasizing the point, in collaboration with the theorist Ignacio Cirac of the Max Planck Institute for Quantum Optics in Garching, Germany, no doubt, competition set aside, is a breakthrough in the field of quantum information and computers, with the potential to transmit and process information how we never dreamt possible. Even this alone, has major implications for healthcare delivery, including access to care, and as Polzik noted, "It is really about teleporting information from one site to another site. Quantum information is different from classical information in the sense that it cannot be measured. It has much higher information capacity and it cannot be eavesdropped on. The transmission of quantum information can be made unconditionally secure." Do these attributes not promise solutions to some of the contentious issues that have held back progress in our efforts to promote the widespread diffusion of healthcare ICT, which would make it easier for us to achieve the dual healthcare delivery goals? Quantum computing essentially needs the manipulation of information embodied in the quantum states of the atoms, including such physical properties as energy, motion, and magnetic field, and as Polzik noted, "Creating entanglement is a very important step but there are two more steps at least to perform teleportation. We have succeeded in making all three steps--that is entanglement, quantum measurement, and quantum feedback," should we not in fact be keen to see this technology develop even further and apply it to healthcare delivery as soon as practicable, which might mean the sort of intersectoral collaboration mentioned earlier in funding relevant projects to move the technology forward? The point here about emerging technology is that of the need to be broad-based in our conceptualization of the issues involved in access to healthcare and the solutions we seek for them. Consideration of emerging technologies in the mix of issues we should analyze is just another dimension of this complex and multifaceted issue, as we have noted repeatedly thus far. There are of course several other potentially useful emerging technologies and many more that we would stumble upon, as we conduct our process cycle analyses, the technologies for the desirable solutions that emerge in the course of which not necessarily already developed. However, we need to have an open mind toward these technologies for us to identify and perhaps discover them. The technology dimension of access to healthcare has a bidirectional relationship to healthcare delivery itself, progress in our efforts at revealing the underlying issues and processes important in improving healthcare delivery including access to health services, likely to involve the revelation of the healthcare information and communication technologies most appropriate to making this happen. The implementation of these technologies, coupled with our ongoing evaluation of a process that is healthcare delivery, subject to perpetual change would in turn likely spawn the need for newer improved technologies. Progress in both healthcare and healthcare information and communication technologies is therefore essentially a symbiotic flux moving us ever closer to the elusive goal of perfection in our delivery of health services. This no doubt, is enough reason for us to continue, as we should to embark on the process cycle analyses mentioned earlier that fuel this dyadic flux. Incidentally, many of the issues that impinge on healthcare delivery also touch these technologies, for example, the issue of privacy and confidentiality of patient information, which because that is patient information that doctors and other healthcare professionals want to access, communicate and share, primarily, we cannot discountenance. It also happens to be the case that technology is crucial to achieving these objectives of safety and confidentiality. Finally, there are legal issues that cut across both domains, to ensure that we assure these objectives, compliance to many for example the Health Insurance Portability and Accountability Act, (HIPAA) necessarily involving the deployment certain types of healthcare ICT under certain circumstances, for example regarding certain types of organizations meeting certain aspects of the Act. This example again illustrates the complexity and interconnectivity of the issues involved in healthcare delivery and healthcare access sometimes. It also exemplifies the need for thoroughness and flexibility in our approaches to addressing these important issues.

To highlight these points even further, as opposed to most other countries,

where publicly funded health systems hold sway, most Americans have some type of private health insurance sponsored by their employers. However, government-sponsored insurance, Medicare, a federal program for those over 65 years of age for example, and a federal/state-sponsored program, Medicaid, essentially for the poor and their families, also play major roles in health insurance in the country. Some contend that this dual health-system arrangement enables the rich with health insurance to access the best quality care, some 45 million Americans with no insurance at all, even experience significant obstacles to care, which further compromises their already fragile health. These are some of the issues and challenges that confront healthcare delivery in the U.S., including compromising access to care solutions to which we need to find and with finding which some of the approaches we have discussed so far could help. In particular, we need to ensure access to care for all, the quality of care delivery equally high at a fundamental level, individuals able to access additional services of their choice, based on their health insurance coverage, or other considerations, such services however, not denied others were they essential aspects of evidence-based best practices for the particular condition in question. Here then, is another crucial dimension of healthcare access that we need to tease out and for which we need to determine the appropriate policies. It is also an instance where the need for the health sector to embrace healthcare information and communication technologies becomes evident. This is because of the need for ongoing updates of the best practices that would form the basis of the fundamental level healthcare provision mentioned above, on the one hand, and for these updates, and indeed, the original practice guidelines to reach the doctors and other healthcare professionals, on the other. It is obvious that such communication needs to be most efficient and the information needs to be available at the point of care, accurately, completely, and in real-time. This also highlights the need for those in the technical domain to develop the required technologies, for example data mining/warehousing and semantic web technologies, and to make them usable in ways that they would enhance rather compromise the productivity of the doctors, lab technologists, and other healthcare professionals using them. To underscore the complexity of the issues that might arise, even with doctors following best practices, consider recent developments in France, where the government, actually just the latest in the series of governments such as Canada,

34

Ireland, Spain, and Norway doing so, announced on October 08, 2006 that it is banning smoking in all public places from February 2007. The fine for breaching the ban would be 75 euros (£50) for individuals and 150 euros for the premises where the offence happened[16]. According to the country's Prime Minister, Mr Dominique de Villepin, who made the announcement in a TV interview, passive smoking kills about 13 people a day in France, which he said was 'unacceptable'. He added, "We started on the basis of a simple observation - two figures: 60,000 deaths a year in our country linked directly to tobacco consumption and 5,000 deaths linked to passive smoking. It is an unacceptable reality in our country in terms of public health." Some would even suggest differential access to care as additional measures for those that will not quit smoking, for example, stipulated payments for some services, an approach implied when Mr de Villepin added the state would take charge of one-third of the costs of anti-smoking treatments, such as a patch, adding, "That would represent the first month of treatment." With opinion polls in France, often deemed a nation of smokers, suggesting that 70% of the people support the ban could such polls influence policy on such differential access to healthcare not just for those that smoke but also that have other conditions for example obesity, in the U.S., down the road? It seems some would argue that part of ensuring access to qualitative care to all involves the care being there in the first place, which means confronting the challenges posed by soaring healthcare costs, which they might contend include discouraging the costs imposed on the health system by such conditions as smoking. On the other hand, others might prefer the investments in additional measures to promote the prevention of smoking by individuals, for example, new healthcare ICT and technology-enabled disease prevention models, for example that would contextual and focus the information conveyed to specific populations, and adapt multimedia quality to the user's device. Indeed, multimedia devices are beginning to proceed into a post-PC era, more of them with the capability to download from the internet, with the emergence of a multi-channel multimedia future, TVs, games consoles, PDAs, mobile phones, and media players, among others becoming mainstream Internet access approaches. These technologies would no doubt have potential applicability for sophisticated healthcare program delivery, including a variety of disease prevention programs including those targeted at cigarette smokers and individuals with obesity among others. Experts predict that in the near future, broadcasters would be able to use the internet protocol (IP) to distribute TV content over cable, ADSL, and wirelessly. Indeed, telephone firms and their clients are already switching to Voice-Over-IP (VoIP) technology, this technology remarkably gaining increasing currency. However, transmission quality, particularly for video, which often use very large files, and bandwidth, could be poor especially on large screens, not to mention storage requirement for large numbers of files, and time to encode the files into the correct bitrates and format. There is also the difficulty providing content to a homeowner whose internet connection is slow, as TV over the internet needs a 4 Mbps connection, rare for example in homes in Europe, the base of the IST-sponsored DANAE project that aims to solve these problems17. The project would develop a new file format that optimizes the quality of the video for a particular device, the format able to deliver to the varieties of present video technology terminals, for examples HDTV and mobile phones, and adapt media content in real-time. Noted project coordinator Renaud Cazoulat, "It means that, for example, the quality of the content improves or reduces as coverage improves or degrades, in the home, it means that bandwidth is shared optimally between all the devices accessing content". The project achieved real-time content adaptation, a technically complicated exercise first holding the content in a master file on a server, adapt it via a media gateway, and then deliver it to the device at the optimum quality for the latter and the local milieu. The media standard, scalable video coding (SVC,) underlies the process, enabling the encoding of video files to facilitate streaming, essentially offering the internet broadcasting counterpart in multiple resolutions. This technology no doubt

36

would be useful for content delivery in the health sector, many chipmakers already keen on developing the microchips by the media gateway to encode the files, and for PDAs, which presently lack the hardware for video coding the DANAE team developed a "bootstrap solution" that encodes files at a specific resolution. The team is indeed looking beyond its original goal of developing scalable video coding, and exploring the development of rich media content, which could utilize video, audio and text to provide information and entertainment in a specific context, the opportunities for healthcare program development and delivery via which are going to be truly profound. These novel technologies, and there are many more, could potentially improve access to health services, and indeed, overall healthcare delivery, facilitating the achievement of the dual healthcare delivery goals. Therefore, they constitute another important dimension requiring in-depth exploration in our quest to facilitate access to care. Furthermore, by so doing, we would be activating the symbiotic healthcare delivery/healthcare ICT dyadic mentioned earlier, motorizing, or otherwise accelerating the evolution of both that would eventually result in progress toward our achieving the dual healthcare delivery objectives, including improving access to health services. As with the other dimensions to the problem of access to care, there is no doubt about the need for and value of process cycle analysis in jump-starting in a manner of speaking, this symbiotic dyadic, starting from either end, for example, with an identified healthcare access issue, such as cigarette smoking, or the uninsured. Implementing changes that would enable Medicare, Medicaid, and Social Security deal with the imminent retirement of baby boomers, expansion of health savings accounts, key to increasing coverage choices and consumers' suaveness in buying healthcare, although some argue that high-deductible plans favor the wealthy and healthy and enables employers to shift healthcare costs to employees, is no doubt important. The question is whether these and other measures are sufficient, in themselves to address the problems they purportedly aim to solve, in particular without the application of health information and communication technologies where necessary. This is because many of these initiatives and others for examples, the AHPs mentioned earlier, HSAs, buying health insurance across states, and medical liability reforms, as diverse as they seem, yet all in one way or another capable of improving access to care and overall healthcare delivery, have underlying processes we could modify using the appropriate healthcare ICT. The ability of the healthcare consumer to make rational choices in purchasing health services, critical to the success of HSAs for example, requires the consumer to have accurate and current data and information that would enable this to happen. How else could she or he acquire such data and information in the most efficient and cost-effective way other than electronically, via content delivery of the sort the novel, and emerging technologies we mentioned earlier could help achieve contextually and customized, enhancing the chances of their reception and utilization? Is this not sufficient reason for example for us to support such projects financially, at least those healthcare stakeholders with the resources so to do? Do AHPs also not need valuable information about healthcare providers to give their members the best advice on which to patronize, and would they not benefit from efficient electronic information flow rather than rely on snail mail to achieve their objectives? Would it not be easier for the consumer to purchase health insurance across states were accurate and reliable information required in making such choices readily available to him or her? Even in capping medial liability in an effort to protect doctors from excessive and frivolous litigation, and the health system from costly defensive practices, could the doctor not in fact prevent any liability in the first place having access at the point of care and in real time to benchmark practices? Given the pervasiveness of health information and communication technologies in contemporary healthcare delivery, including improving access to care, should we not in fact pay more attention to promoting their diffusion in the health sector, and would this not make it easier for us to achieve the dual healthcare delivery goals mentioned earlier? The answers to these questions many would consider obvious, yet it seems that the health industry continues to struggle embracing these technologies to the extent that it should, for a variety of reasons that range from costs to technophobia. All of these however, point to the need for conducting proper and thorough process cycle analyses. It is not only easier to make people see the reason for a particular course of action that way, but also to engage them in implementing the technologies from the start, which the analyses revealed are the solutions to particular issues and problems that a jurisdiction's health system confronts, in regarding access to care or any other healthcare delivery element. This engagement brings us to another important dimension in improving healthcare access, that of the need for end-user buy-in of the technologies that achieving these goals need, or indeed, of any system's changes required. This is perhaps the most important aspect of whatever solution we determine and is one we ought to take just as seriously as the solutions themselves. Achieving this end-user buy-in might in fact require the involvement of change management consultants depending on the scope of the project and the resources available for that purpose. Nonetheless, whether internally organized or outsourced, it is important to carry the end-user of the proposed changes along right from the start, as it is clearly futile implementing technologies, which no one would embrace or utilize. Besides, we should aim for these technologies to establish the symbiotic dyadic with our healthcare delivery efforts, as indicated earlier, in a forward motion of continuous improvement of both that would benefit our cause in the long term, that of improving healthcare access and the overall healthcare delivery process.

The multiple dimensions from which we should view our efforts at solving

the problem of access to healthcare in the U.S. reflect the complexities of the issues and processes involved in healthcare delivery itself. Beyond this however, they attest to the need for a thorough and determined multi-level analyses of these issues and processes. As we noted earlier, an important element of the implementation of the outcomes of these analyses is striking a balance between competition and collaboration, a tussle that would surface, again, at all levels and that could involve individuals and/or organizations, besides the issues themselves. In a recent four-day series, titled "The General and the Beast" that Detroit news ran in late September 2006[18], which looked at the consequences of increased health care costs on General Motors (GM). The first in the series examines how GM spends $5.3 billion yearly on health care costs, for about 1.1 million employees, retirees and their families, warning that GM's "health care crisis" be symptomatic of America's in the years ahead. Indeed, the GM issue highlights the need to strike the competition/collaboration balance mentioned above, as we ask ourselves if we should take measures that would run a company such as the GM essentially aground with the potential loss of millions of American jobs, were the company to become uncompetitive at home let alone on the global market. We should also ask ourselves why is that GM despite its substantial investments in efforts intent on curtailing soaring healthcare costs while not compromising access and the quality of health services to its employees continue to struggle in achieving these goals. From cajoling doctors and drug companies, to building the largest wellness education program in the country, and to convincing workers to pay more for medical care, and hospitals to improve efficiencies in ERs, the company has taken several measures that seem not to be working, but why? No one should expect the answer to be easy but should expect to find some of them at least conducting the process cycle analyses we have mentioned so much in our discussion here. By applying the answers coupled with a determination to sustain the competition/collaboration balance, we would no doubt be moving closer to solving the problems we set out to, in the main. To underscore this point, the tradeoff between unemployment and inflation termed the Phillips Curve, held sway in the Economics zeitgeist in the 1950s and 1960s, in other words, that reduced unemployment resulted in a one-time rise in the inflation rate. However, Columbia University Professor, Edmund S. Phelps won the 2006 Nobel Prize in Economics positing that due to persons having incomplete information/knowledge about the actions of others, they have to predicate their decisions on expectations. Stabilization policy could attenuate short-term fluctuations in unemployment, but Phelps noted that current low inflation results in expectations of future low inflation. His ideas, which led to better inflation control has implications for the negative effects of information asymmetry in healthcare delivery, for example in compromising the effectiveness of consumer-driven healthcare, and in our lack of understanding, at least in full, why the measures taken by GM do not seem to be working in the firm achieving its healthcare goals. Thus, as with GM, the need for process cycle analyses is crucial to the revelations derivable from the decomposition and exposition exercises, and required to address the many issues involved successfully. It is also important for the applications of the revelations made during these exercises, which by the way should be ongoing, in tandem with considerations of the competition/collaboration balance to obtain the best results in our efforts to solve salient healthcare delivery problems. Why would a group of doctors want their practices walloped for example by their competitors listening to GM, a collaboration that would be possible were they not to consider that doing so would jeopardize the very existence of their practices? The same goes for the drug companies, and even the workers, and indeed, all the other players in the healthcare delivery mix in which the firm participates. In other words, the decisions based on defective information would be just as defective, perpetuating a cycle of defectiveness that would as is the case with GM, have little effect in the desired direction, that is would unlikely reduce the increasing healthcare costs that is crippling the company, or in the case of the country, its health system. Because this situation is likely to worsen due to the country's aging population, and in particular as millions of baby-boomer retire, it is only apt that we focus on these issues now and find the appropriate solutions to them. It is again clear that we could have a generic approach to tackling the healthcare access and other problems confronting the U.S., health system, but at the end of the day, the solutions would have to come from thorough multi-level analyses, by health jurisdictions, companies, states, and indeed, the entire country.

References

1. Available at:
~~http://www.medicalpost.com/medicine/clinical/article.jsp?content=20061004_~~
122324_2748 Accessed on October 4, 2006

2. Available at:
http://news.yahoo.com/s/hsn/20061005/hl_hsn/studyspotsthebrainsselfishne
~~ssoffswitch&printer=1;_ylt=Ali0QbhPP0M4nPho5OHEVOC9j7AB;_ylu=X3oDM~~
TA3MXN1bHE0BHNlYwN0bWE- Accessed on October 05, 2006

3. Biederman J, Faraone SV, Keenan K, Knee D, Tsuang MT. Family-genetic and psychosocial risk factors in DSM-III attention deficit disorder. J Am Acad Child Adolesc Psychiatry. 1990; 29:526-533.

4. Faraone SV, Biederman J, Keenan K, Tsuang MT. A family-genetic study of girls with DSM-III attention deficit disorder. Am J Psychiatry. 1991; 148:112-117.

5. Available at:
http://www.nytimes.com/2006/10/01/business/yourmoney/01drug.html?_r=
2&ref=yourmoney&oref=slogin&oref=slogin Accessed on October 5, 2006

6. Available at: http://www.nsf.gov/ Accessed on October 05, 2006

7. Available at: http://www.nih.gov/news/pr/oct2006/od-02.htm Accessed on October 6, 2006

8. Available at: http://www.nsf.gov/news/news_summ.jsp?cntn_id=108067 Accessed on October 6, 2006

43

9. Available at:

http://news.yahoo.com/s/ap/20061006/ap_on_go_ca_st_pe/budget_deficit&p rinter=1;_ylt=AvLBBUkxq5dg1hywFcqfokOWwvIE;_ylu=X3oDMTA3MXNlbH E0BHNlYwN0bWE-
Accessed on October 06, 2006

10. Available at: www.oecd.org/health/healthdata. Accessed on October 7, 2006

11. Available at: http://www.washingtonpost.com/wp-

dyn/content/article/2006/04/04/AR2006040401937.html
Accessed on October 7, 2006

12. Available at:

http://www.nytimes.com/2006/10/08/washington/08health.html?_r=1&oref= slogin
Accessed October 8, 2006

13. Available at: http://library.ahima.org/xpedio/
Accessed on October 8, 2006

14. Available at: http://edworkforce.house.gov/issues/108th/recess/ahps.htm
Accessed on October 8, 2006

15. Available at: http://news.com.com/2102-11395_3-
6122801.html?tag=st.util.print Accessed on October 8, 2006

16. Available at: http://news.bbc.co.uk/2/hi/europe/6032125.stm Accessed on
October 9, 2006

17. Available at:

http://istresults.cordis.tu/index.cfm/section/news/tpl/article/BrowsingType/
Features/ID/88626 Accessed on October 9, 2006

18. Available at:

http://detnews.com/apps/pbcs.dll/section?Category=LIFESTYLE03&template
=HEALTHCARECRISIS
Accessed on October 9, 2006

Healthcare in the U.S. and the
Competition-Collaboration Conundrum

The recent call in the October 10, 2006 *New England Journal of Medicine*

editorial, to the U.S. Food and Drug Administration (FDA) to implement without delay the recommendations of a recent Institute of Medicine (IOM) report on the safety of new prescription drugs in the U.S., is instructive vis-à-vis improving the U.S health system. Safety issues regarding prominent prescription medications in the country have been topical in recent times, some of these medications, for example, Merck's painkiller Vioxx, eventually withdrawn, although the 'crisis of confidence' they generated in the public, lingers on. The report, issued at FDA's request in September 2006 by the IOM Committee on the Assessment of the United States Drug Safety System noted that the FDA currently is unable to ensure the safety of new prescription drugs for a number of reasons, including inadequate funds, cultural and structural problems, and "unclear and insufficient regulatory authorities". Among the recommendations made in the report for FDA to improve prescription drug safety, limitations on direct-to-consumer advertising of new drugs, augmented post-market review, and special new drugs labeling featured prominently. Indeed, the editorial urges swift action in establishing a stronger system of drug regulation with the IOM report serving as a "crucial starting point". Noted FDA spokesperson Julie Zawisza in responding, "FDA believes it is important that public discussions on drug safety take place, and we welcome the input from people across the government and within the health care and health policy communities." She added, "All drugs have risks, and the challenge is for FDA to uncover them sooner and to improve its tools for communicating these risks to the public". The issues the report and the editorial raised and those that the FDA response likely would in some quarters underscore the complex relationships of the fundamental elements of the competition and collaboration conundrum that pervades health systems worldwide, and whose flavors across the American healthcare landscape we would explore in our discussion here. Our exploration would serve an exposition heuristics in tandem with a prescriptive, whose potential for generating the sort of fresh perspectives scaling the odds seemingly atavistic and acquired in the American health system, another example, let us say the outbreak of an influenza pandemic, would help further highlight. On May 11, 2006, the 1996 Physiology/Medicine Nobel laureate Peter Doherty at a lecture at MIT titled "Plagues, Pestilences and Influenza", noted that it would require a mix of scientific work and political planning to tackle such a situation effectively. Thus, were scientists even to create an effective vaccine, it would still be important not only to produce enough for all that needs it, but also to expect huge challenges distributing it efficiently, for example, the inter-organization that this latter would entail likely to cut across competitive spectra, even within the same organization or sector. Observed Doherty, "These are not simply scientific problems, it's really a matter of policy and logistics," and with the potential for the sprouting perhaps without warning, of a novel infectious disease as did severe acute respiratory syndrome (SARS) in 2002/03, the need for resolving the competition/collaboration conundrum comes into sharp focus, in particular in an increasingly global world2. This is doubtless so as not elucidating the cause of the disease and its effective treatment promptly could potentially be catastrophic, that a strain of avian flu, H1N1 thought to cause the 1918-1919 influenza pandemic killed 40 million people worldwide, a pointer to the havoc these bugs, including the much talked-about current avian flu strain, H5N1, could wreck on humankind. Worse still, the mid-C14th bubonic plague outbreak in Europe, exterminated a third of the continent's peoples. In particular, if the novel flu was deadliest in young adults, as the 1918 was, due to a swift immune response, the "cytokine storm" it triggered that typically results in blood leakage and shock, with as Doherty noted "People essentially (drowning) in their own body fluids," the economic consequences among others would, some would surmise, unimaginable. It is even more troubling to have to wager between one long-drawn-out pandemic scenario versus a swift devastating one, which latter as with young adults mostly affected that results in the rapid burnout of the pandemic with the hosts dead, because we have not sufficiently, if at all contemplated the significance of and resolved the competition/collaboration conundrum. This resolution would be multidimensional involving an in-depth understanding of the underlying issues, in our efforts to prevent emerging microbes, for examples, the role animal hosts play in their transition to humans, and those of population growth, town and city planning, air travel, and of health education and promotion, among others. On health education/promotion for example, McGinnis and Foege, comparing the ten foremost diagnoses, versus actual causes of death in the U.S in 1990, noted, "If the nation is to achieve its full potential for better health, public policy must focus directly and actively on those factors that represent the root determinants of death and disability."3 They also observed that behavioral choices, not genetic or external factors, accounted for half of deaths, hence public health education and prevention interventions could help prevent them. In exploring the competition/collaboration conundrum

(CCC), say regarding public health priorities, costs would be a key consideration, indeed the determinant, quite often, even stripped of any ethico-moral underlay, of the outcome of the CCC. U.S spending on public health emergency preparedness for examples, new epidemics, bioterrorism, and natural disasters, among others, in 2003 was $1.6 billion for bio-terrorism preparedness to state and local governments [4], in whose charge is public health primarily, yearly grants about $1.3 billion thereafter. Even with influenza pandemic preparedness now featuring more in contemporary public health emergency strategies, versus the $5.9 billion the federal government gives the states yearly for all other public health initiatives, and the states' $10-$15 billion annual expenditures on public health[6] , spending on emergency-preparedness initiatives, 6% to 8% of total yearly spending on public health, remains contentious. Is the U.S spending too much on public health emergency preparedness as some experts contend, paying less attention to disease prevention, preventable diseases responsible for 50% of the 2.5 million persons that die in the U.S., annually? That the CCC is operational even within the same domain as this example shows points to the importance of this dyadic and how its resolution is a crucial aspect of efforts to improve the U.S health system, and indeed, of any other worldwide. This includes, as we will show in our discussion here, countries with publicly funded health systems, where the competitive forces operational in whose health systems might not be immediately obvious. We will also show the significant role that healthcare information and communication technologies appropriately deployed could play in resolving the conundrum, and in improving the U.S., health system as a result. Indeed, research evidence increasingly indicates that these technologies could improve healthcare delivery, and facilitate the achievement of the dual healthcare delivery objectives of qualitative healthcare delivery simultaneously reducing health spending. The European Commission published the eHealth IMPACT study in September 2006, in "eHealth is Worth it – The economic benefits of implemented eHealth solutions at ten European sites[7], which gave empirical support to the substantial health, economic and social benefits derivable from the implementation of healthcare ICT. As Vivian Reding, European Commissioner for Information Society and media noted in the publication, "The eHealth market is currently some 2% of total healthcare expenditure in Europe, but has the potential to more than double in size, almost reaching the volume of the market for medical devices or half the size of the pharmaceuticals market. However, unlike the products from these two other healthcare industries, eHealth applications are not yet routinely assessed for their impact, benefits, and safety." These latter, the study has to a major extent done, the benefits for example ranging from "improvements in quality and better access of all citizens to care, to avoidance of unnecessary cost to the public purse", further noted Reding, determined via a generic methodology for the economic appraisal of eHealth applications. This essentially was a context adaptive model, which therefore matches diverse applications, clinical settings, administrative operations, supply chain solutions, and the like, and predicates on cost-benefit analysis[7]. It also considered costs as total costs of ownership (TCO), even highlighted the idea of cost-avoidance, in this instance the prohibitive costs of achieving the ICT-based performance without ICT. According to the study, effective healthcare ICT investment result in improved productivity and quality of care that help optimize capacity facilitate access to care, the value of these benefits for a "virtual health economy", post the development and implementation stages of the technologies, increasing annually and outpacing costs, typically quite substantially. The study also noted the relative stability of yearly costs after implementation, versus the continual growth of net benefits annually with expanded use, further improving healthcare delivery and increasing the prospects of the health system achieving the dual healthcare delivery objectives, the costs vis-à-vis benefits of implementing these technologies shown in Figure 1.

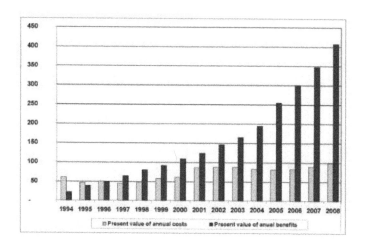

Year	

Legend: ☐ Present value of annual costs   ■ Present value of anual benefits

$\mathbf{I}$t is ironical that despite this and similar evidence of the qualitative and

quantitative benefits of the widespread diffusion and utilization of healthcare information and communication technologies, the health industry, which generates information literally by the second, is still painfully slow in adopting these technologies. A study released on October 11, 2006 for example observed that only roughly 25% of doctors use some form of electronic health records (EHR), in the U.S., and less than 1 in 10 use such records effectively. This means their use for examples as an element of an overall health information system that gathers patient information collects and shows lab-tests results, involved in decision-making, in e-prescribing and in other documentations. This compromises the chances of the realization of President Bush's goal for EHR coverage for most Americans by 2014, although the study noted that more doctors each year are adopting these technologies. The above examples buttress the point we made earlier regarding resolving the CCC being an important aspect of any efforts to improve healthcare delivery in America, and indeed, elsewhere. The tension between competition and collaboration manifests in various guises as the examples also show, but beneath the veneer is always a push-and-pull phenomenon that regarding healthcare delivery in particular, and indeed, any other process-laden enterprise, the implementation of the appropriate information and communication technologies could help ease. Underlying the implementation of these technologies is another, in fact more important exercise, one on which depends, the recognition of which technologies are appropriate in a particular instance, the process analysis cycle. In the U.S., for example, it is hardly that the benefits of healthcare ICT are unknown, and many actively promote their widespread adoption. On the other hand are privacy advocates, determined to block the widespread use of these technologies, here again, the need to acknowledge the basis for the competition between the two crucial for us to work out that for collaboration between them. The outcome of this exercise for example could be the development of cutting-edge healthcare ICT that would guarantee the privacy and confidentiality of patient information that the latter so yearns for. Noted Deborah C. Peel, a psychiatrist and founder of Patient Privacy Rights, an Austin-based nonprofit privacy advocate for example, "The big problem is that the vast majority of electronic medical-record systems do not give patients the right to decide who has access to the records...They do not give patients the right to segment sensitive portions. . . . The electronic medical records in use now have been designed primarily for the convenience of physicians." The study found that 5-10% of U.S. hospitals use computerized physician order entry (CPOE), city doctors embrace healthcare ICT more than rural doctors, and those in the West more than those in the South, Midwest, and Northeast. It also found that doctors practicing alone or with one other doctor were much less likely to implement EHR, a key finding since almost 50% of U.S. doctors fit into this category, costs, and disruption in customary ways of work among the reasons to which the researchers attributed the slow adoption of healthcare ICT. There are however, potentially more, technophobia, fear of litigation, lack of technological infrastructure, regulatory barriers, loss of status, defective, or lack of end-user buy-in, lack of technical standards and related issues such as interoperability, and security issues, among them. Again, underlying all these issues are potential conflicts, or competing interests, which therefore stand in the way of the collaboration we need to secure the implementation of these technologies for the health system to benefit from their immense potential. In other words, the adoption of the CCC model in tackling the issues and problems that confront the U.S., health system would serve a variety of purposes depending on the scope of the concept adopted in particular circumstances. Regardless of the scope however, the model enables us identify the issues that need further in-depth analyses, which would reveal the dynamics of the competing forces and the approaches to resolving these forces for them to operate in tandem to result in the desired outcome, the delivery of qualitative health services, cost-effectively. These analyses, which would essentially constitute a decomposition/exposition, or process cycle analyses, would in turn reveal the appropriate healthcare information and communication technologies that we would need to facilitate the achievement of these goals. In fact, they would do much more, as it would then be possible for us in strengthening collaboration between these hitherto competing forces, to identify the healthcare ICT that would actually be "constitutive", sort of embedded into the mechanics of the operations that lead to the desired results, motorizing them perpetually in the direction of continuous quality improvement. These exercises, on the aggregate would by improving every process involved in the realization of the desired outcome, help us in achieving the dual healthcare delivery goals. There are numerous instances of inter-organizational collaboration in the U.S. health system. For example, seven U.S. medical centers via a federal grant announced on October 10, 2006, will soon establish the first collaborative electronic database of HIV/AIDS treatment results. This would no doubt help evaluate the effectiveness of treatments given HIV-positive individuals. The medical centers are the University of Alabama at Birmingham, Case Western Reserve University; Harvard University; Johns Hopkins University; University of California-San Diego; University of California-San Francisco; and University of Washington. These centers currently run HIV/AIDS treatment databases, which the project plans to connect facilitating communication and information sharing among doctors and researchers, hence comparative analyses of the effectiveness of frequently used HIV/AIDS therapeutic modalities versus the results of clinical trials for novel drugs. According to Michael Saag, principal investigator for the project, the $2.45 million grant from the National Institute of Allergy and Infectious Disease and the National Heart, Lung and Blood Institute would enable the addition of five more centers to the network9. This example illustrates the potential benefits derivable from extending competition into the collaborative domain. The key issue here is not necessarily to replace competition with collaboration, but to merge the two. In other words, part of the problem with the U.S. health system is not establishing this tipping point, the various elements of the system in essentially an undeclared warfare, most times, their activities not favorable to the achievement of the dual healthcare delivery goals. Some would no doubt argue that this is not the reason many of these elements are in business, but it would on scrutiny, emerge as one that is crucial to their businesses to survive, let alone thrive. Is it any wonder then that the European Commission for example is introducing to be operational in 2007, a resource named Open Source Observatory and Repository (OSOR) for public sector organizations to share open-source code and applications? The goals of OSOR, established as part of efforts to promote the adoption of open source technology among EU member states, include improving the return on investment of open-source projects and to facilitate interoperability among applications. Are these goals not sine qua non achieving the dual healthcare delivery objectives, the former encouraging investments in the technologies that would help in so doing, the latter facilitating the technologies in so doing? Aimed purely at the public sector, the EC expects it to succeed, as many similar projects already exist across the EU, OSOR itself an extension of the current Open Source Observatory Web portal, a repository of source and object code and information on the utilization of applications, licenses, and contract documents, added. Would the goals of OSOR not benefit health systems, most in fact reliant on public funding in the EU, specifically in their quest to achieve the dual healthcare delivery goals? Is this as the earlier example not evidence of the transition from competition to collaboration yielding ample dividends and capable of facilitating the realization of the goals of healthcare delivery crucial to the survival of health systems in contemporary times? Noted Karel De Vriendt, head of the EU's e-government services unit, actively involved in the project, "The new OSOR should become the preferred cooperation tool to speed up software pooling among Member States," which no doubt would have a similar effect on the achievement of the dual healthcare delivery goals, albeit in the long term. Google, which has also established a substitute resource, a repository for programmers to host software projects, GoogleCode, facilitates discussions as with the EC project, but not under every open-source license. That Google joined the OpenDocument Format Alliance (ODF) is significant, and indicates the potentially rosy future of this technology, in particular as major IT firms such as IBM, and Sun Microsystems, among others support it too, besides key government clients in Belgium, Denmark, and Massachusetts, and Microsoft, which recently initiated the Open XML Translator project. Microsoft's project enables developers to create software capable of converting Microsoft Office documents to OpenDocument, hence makes it possible to open/save them in the OpenDocument Format. Indeed, the company on October 23, 2006 plans to release the converter that will enable Word users open documents saved in the OpenDocument format, this pug-in for word, its first initiative in its support for the ODF standard, a first prototype of the "Save to ODF" Word add-on expected out also in late October 2006. In 2007, the Open XML Translator project that the French firm, Clever Age, handles plans to build converters able to translate between Microsoft's Excel and PowerPoint and the analogous ODF file formats. Other ODF-to-Office-Open-XML conversion projects are in progress, one from the OpenDocument Foundation included. ODF exemplifies the collaborative spirit even among competitors that needs to pervade the U.S. health system to ensure its continual improvement. To garner support from government clients, Microsoft for example, wants to standardize Office Open XML at the European standards groups Ecma International and the International Standards Organization (ISO,) its approval as a standard by the Ecma General Assembly expected in December 2006, after which it goes to ISO. Novell and Apple Computer representatives at the assembly also suggested amendments to the documentation that would enable the formats operate with non-Windows operating systems (OS) and with different programming languages. We should mention though that not all industry key players are joining in, for example, IBM, which contends that Ecma would be merely "rubber-stamping" Microsoft's existing Office Open XML specification as standard. Nonetheless, the involvement of these technology titans in ODF further confirms the potential for competition and collaboration to blend seamlessly for the achievement of the common good.

Governments are also interested in ODF as earlier noted. Recently a French

MP prepared a report for Prime Minister Dominique de Villepin recommending that France mandate the use of the OpenDocument format, or ODF. The MP also recommended France "propose to its European partners to systematically favor open standards and, as the first example, to mandate the international ISO format ODF for the creation and diffusion of all official document exchange at the European level." The fact that no single vendor controls it, that free and open-source software offer economic benefits to particularly small businesses, and cost savings to governments explains, among other reasons, why ODF is gaining currency in the public and private sectors alike. The above examples underscore the need as earlier noted for us to re-conceptualize the terms competition and collaboration to make them as inclusive as possible in addressing the problems that the U.S. health system confronts. Again, as we have noted, humankind has the capacity to collaborate, but is also intuitively competitive, not to mention the forces, natural and manmade, some individual, others organization-related, that tend to exacerbate these tendencies. The foray of the core ideas of consumerism into the health sector for example, is influencing every facet of the latter, competitiveness one of these core concepts, and in influencing the nature and type of healthcare information and communication technologies that emerge in the sector, it would, approaches to healthcare delivery in the future. In other words, we would be even under more pressure to find a meeting point between the forces of competition and of collaboration in the years ahead, caught as it were between our acknowledgement of the biological/evolutionary basis of both and of the exigencies of our contemporary times. As with how it often is, left with little if any choice in dealing with such conflicts in other domains of our existence, the outcome of our decision itself could be crucial to our very existence that these basic tendencies strive to preserve. The economy of most of the world doubtless has democratic underpinnings that nurture our competitive instincts. In healthcare delivery, this manifests increasingly in the right of the healthcare consumer to choose service providers and to engage actively in the healthcare delivery process, among others. This consumer-driven healthcare, which is gaining increasing currency in the U.S. and elsewhere, is a natural progression of the freedom from other domains of our lives that we enjoy and so much cherish. However, as a secondary process, it also, with the optimal operations of competitive market forces, helps create the enabling environment for the achievement of the dual healthcare delivery objectives. In fact, it is the combination of this freedom to choose, and the effective operations of market forces that make the term, consumer-driven, meaningful. In other words, we need to ensure the two remain unfettered for us to achieve the ideals of the consumer-driven healthcare model. This is why it is incompatible with this endeavor to thwart competition. Indeed, it is why we need to promote competition, which would in certain instances, bring us in direct collision with any effort at collaboration, which underscores the need to focus on the appropriate ways to resolve any CCC we identify, were we to progress in improving healthcare delivery in the country, considering the crucial role collaboration plays in this regard. We need to find ways to harness the forces of competition and blend them with those of collaboration to attain the desired results. Starting with competition for example, in a health system in which the consumer-driven healthcare delivery model is operational, such as in the U.S., we need to understand how the competitive forces involved interplay with one another firstly. We mentioned earlier for example that the healthcare consumer is at the center of such a model that in exercising the freedom to choose would no doubt have expectations commensurate with the particular consumer's knowledge and understanding of the variety of issues involved in the healthcare delivery process. This knowledge would at once liberate and empower the healthcare consumer, regarding managing his or her health affairs. In addition, it would make the healthcare consumer more discerning, making more informed choices, on the one hand cost saving, and on the other, ensuring the receipt of high quality healthcare. The healthcare consumer is thus, achieving the dual healthcare delivery goals on a different, albeit personal level, than say government, which seeks to achieve similar objectives. In fact, by so doing, the individual healthcare consumer is making it easier for government to do so too. Part of the individual achieving these objectives imply stimulating competition among healthcare providers who, in meeting the heightened expectations of the healthcare consumer would need to enhance its value propositions to the consumer, which would invariably involve implementing and deploying cutting-edge healthcare ICT to deliver programs that offer it the competitive edge it needs to perhaps even survive. The consumer would, in the healthcare delivery equation of the future be able to articulate the healthcare ICT that it expects chosen healthcare providers to have. Health consumers would, in dictating the pace of say healthcare information and communication technologies implementation by healthcare providers, also be helping propel the progress of healthcare delivery, improvements in which deploying such technologies would likely result. Thus, the healthcare consumer would become an engine literally for the realization of the symbiotic dyadic between healthcare delivery and these technologies, progress in one likely leading to progress in the other, each essentially feeding into the other in a perpetual quality improvement process. This quality improvement at different levels of healthcare delivery, which is also measurable, and which we should in fact do, is the main ingredient for the achievement of the dual healthcare delivery objectives in the overall health system of the country. It is therefore important that we do not muzzle competition, and we should in fact promote such healthcare delivery models as would stimulate and nurture it. It is possible to argue that such healthcare delivery models as the consumer-driven healthcare favor one group or another, say government and the wealthy, but as we have noted it is not enough to foster competition, we must prevent it colliding with collaboration, and in fact, we should nurture both. It would then become evident that the goals we want to achieve, the dual healthcare delivery goals, which as we saw earlier is achievable at different levels, would benefit all one way or another. No one would likely blame state and local governments in the U.S for embarking on reforming spending, whose debts as bonds were about $1.9 trillion in 2005, and whose pension plans are underfunded by about $700 billion, their retiree health benefits, according to some estimates, by $1.4 trillion countrywide[11], the potential effects on taxpayers, among others stark. New Jersey for example projected an 18% annual growth over four years of spending on its employee health plan, which already has a $20 billion unfunded retiree benefits pile-up[12]. It would also unlikely be surprising that Michigan and Alaska now embrace savings-based or defined-contribution pension plans in place of customary pension/retiree health plans, for new workers, who would essentially prefund their retirements, and would likely be even more discerning in their lifestyle and healthcare provider choices. Would anyone chide these states under the prevailing fiscal circumstances for adopting such reform measures, as others likely would to reduce munificent retirement benefits in particular with states enduring the most of these benefits versus the private sector, most likely health benefits for current workers, since slashing pension benefits for this group could legally be more complicated? With the imminent retirement of baby-boomers, the questions raised by these issues would likely to be central to future public health and fiscal policies, for example, that of the prospects of tax hikes, versus say savings-based retirement plans, considering the problems the former could spawn for the global competitiveness of the U.S economy, among others. Would compelling the private sector to boost their retiree pensions and health plans for example, be compromising the collaboration it might otherwise be prepared to offer in other critical aspects of the healthcare delivery process, albeit simply because of diversion of the resources they intended to use in a different direction? Furthermore, would it in fact also compromise their ability to maintain their workforce, much more engage new ones, resulting in layoffs and an increasingly large numbers of idle persons, and make these firms less competitive on the world stage? Here again, not only is the interrelatedness of health and economic forces evident, but so is that of the need to strike a reasonable balance between competition and collaboration rather than favor one to the exclusion of the other. It is this balancing act that would characterize the health system of the future with the potential to succeed in achieving the dual healthcare delivery goals, which achievement would be important in determining the survival or otherwise of these health systems. Because it is important to both the individual healthcare consumer, health systems, and other healthcare stakeholders to achieve the dual healthcare delivery goals, with regard the health systems, for example, due to the soaring health spending at all health jurisdictional levels, including besides the state/local governments levels exemplified above, at the federal level, achieving this balance is crucial.

Developments in the information and communication technologies domain

would increasingly drive the achievement of this balance, including but not limited to those in Web 2.0, or second-generation Internet-based services with collaboration technologies such as wikis, blogs, folksonomies, social networking sites, and programmable Web sites, which enable users to create mashup applications. Mashups for example, are not complicated endeavors as they utilize conventional Web technologies, REST/POX and scripting languages, mashups veritable sources of novelty and distinctiveness to content that could garner competitive advantage. These technologies also underscore the increasing relevance of the "open source"/collaborative mode in the emergent information technology space whose impact would ricochet right through the multifarious elements involved in healthcare delivery in the years ahead. It would be commoner for example for us to see even in the health sector, the use of AJAX (Asynchronous JavaScript and XML), an approach to creating interactive Web applications, to extract competitive market edge, driven by the demand by the increasingly suave healthcare consumer for health services whose efficient and const-effective delivery healthcare ICT would likely best assure. In essence, the encroachment as some would contend of the core ideals of consumerism into the health sector would reach full cycle, giving the healthcare provider with little choice than to embrace the concept of striking the right balance between competition and collaboration to survive. Paradoxically, this quest for survival is not just of the individual healthcare provider, but also that of the entire health system, which if moribund, would inevitably take many such providers along. The point here is that the health sector has to be attuned to its changing milieu, and acquire the appropriate mindset, so to say, in an evolving world wherein the outcome of the interplay of the healthcare information and communication technologies and healthcare delivery dyadic has the potential to help us achieve the dual healthcare delivery goals. Vendors would also increasingly adapt Web 2.0 technologies in products and services targeted at the healthcare industry, in response to the demands of the healthcare consumer on the one hand and the provider on the other. An appreciation of market needs, vertical or horizontal, would come from these vendors also engaging in process cycle analyses of their markets of interest. IBM, for example, whose forte is marketing to businesses, recently released QEDwiki, aimed at allowing individuals to assemble Web applications utilizing wikis, really simple syndication (RSS) and simple Web scripting. Whichever segment of the healthcare delivery process they wish to consider, medical specialty, demographics, gender, location, and so on, a thorough appraisal of the issues involved would be key to determining the most appropriate technologies the segment requires, now and in future. In other words, process cycle analysis is a tool that anyone or firm interested to better understand and help resolve the issues that confront the U.S or any health system would find invaluable. With the user at the center of the healthcare delivery universe, understanding how the deployment of the right healthcare information and communication technologies could improve health services delivery to him or her is going to yield ample dividends also for the software and other ICT vendors. In fact, some experts contend that the seeming disconnect between organization and consumer software design, would have to change, in particular the adoption by many companies of the so-called service-oriented architecture (SOA), a modular system design they argue the much more user-friendly Web 2.0 technologies would in time torpedo. Even IBM, one of SOA's key proponents is showing interests in these latter technologies as mentioned earlier, its QEDwiki project specifically aimed at enabling corporate-world individuals with no programming skills put together "mashups". These "mashups" are applications that could collate multi-sourced information. This makes it possible for example, to track the nature, extent, effect, and any other information of a nocosomial infection in a health facility by combining information from a variety of sources within the facility, nurses, house cleaners, doctors, lab technicians, patients, and outside it, for example, current literature, and information from other facilities. There are no doubt obstacles in the way of the widespread adoption of Web 2.0 technologies in the health sector, not least because of the privacy and confidentiality issues most crucial to health information sharing, and some are considering the security risks involved and the chances of hacking into the information systems of health facilities. These are quite serious concerns but are surmountable, nor is the arrival of Web 2.0 necessarily indicative of the demise of enterprise software. In fact, Microsoft is also recently seeking areas of overlap among Web 2.0, SOAs, and software as a service, sponsoring a workshop in March 2006, termed Spark, at its Mix '06 conference, aimed at finding common technical-design patterns applicable to business and consumer software. This is the sort of blending of competition with collaboration that would eventually emerge as the way forward in our approaches to addressing the challenges the U.S health system and indeed, all other health systems worldwide face. The context in which these health systems operate would determine the finer details of the mechanisms for forging this balance, but nonetheless, each health system would need to do so, to create the necessary opportunities that solving the often hydra-headed challenges contemporary health systems confront demands. We have emphasized the role that healthcare information and communication technologies would play in solving these problems not because these technologies constitute the exclusive solutions to the problems of the U.S., health systems, but because they are critical to improving the processes that underlie the issues involved. It might not be quite straightforward for example, to see the connection between these technologies and the Medicare Part D, a federal program aimed at absorbing the costs of prescription drugs for Medicare beneficiaries and part of the Medicare Prescription Drug, Improvement, and Modernization Act of 2003 (MMA), started on January 1,2006. Yet, when one considers the numbers of seniors that were unable to access these prescriptions, the worsening of their ailments that would result, and the risks of death some faced due to, among others, let us for simplicity say, the "computer glitch" the sudden information surge the program's initiation caused, the link would likely be clearer. Consider another example, small businesses are taking an increasing share of U.S. employment, which itself might at first seem benign until one considers the potential adverse consequences of this trend for health care coverage of millions of American workers. Latest government statistics indicate that small firms employed 50.9% of private-sector employees in 2004, versus 50.7% in 2003, the increase, three years in a row. With more Americans working for small firms, though, are less chances that they would receive medical coverage and other benefits, for example, retirement plans, since these firms are less likely to offer the benefits, evident in 60% of firms with three to 199 employees offering health benefits in 2006, as opposed to 98% of those with 200 or more employees. With small firms often in service industries, which require more workers than automation, and big firms in manufacturing with increasing likelihood for automation hence more prone to layoffs, particularly during economic downturns, should we not factor these trends in our efforts to resolve the CCC and improve our prospects of achieving the dual healthcare delivery goals? Both small and big firms are in business to make profits, which might some way or another conflict with measures they take that would result in collaborating with other stakeholders in achieving the dual healthcare delivery goals. Reminding them of the big picture, which they probably know but perhaps deny or consider a secondary concern, which is that making profits, and indeed, their very survival are tied together with the achievement of these dual healthcare delivery goals, is important but should perhaps come next to measures more likely to make immediate sense to them. These measures for example would make it likelier for small firms to offer healthcare benefits to their employees, and large firms, not implode under pressure from health benefits crippling their businesses and sending their employees into the ranks of the unemployed. Here is where healthcare information and communication technologies come in. Would these firms, both small and large, chief among whose reasons for having issues with offering health benefits are costs, not be better able to offer them were these benefits to cost less, and their employees stay healthier? Would these costs not be less were their employees to be more discerning in their choices of healthcare providers, and indeed, lifestyles? Is providing their employees with the relevant information that would enable them make rational choices not the first step in ensuring that they do? Would such information not make it less likely for them to have medical examinations, lab investigations, and surgical procedures, even medications, whose prices are not competitive, or that they do not even need, or could have used less expensive ones? How could encouraging these firms to promote healthy lifestyles help keep their employees healthy and reduce healthcare costs? The answers to these questions are doubtless important reasons for incorporating healthcare information and communication technologies into these firms' efforts at providing their employees and retirees qualitative health services, cost-effectively. These technologies, implemented at various levels would facilitate rectifying the information asymmetry common in the health sector, making the right information, for example on pricing of procedures, on generic medications that are just as effective as brand ones, and on health and wellness in general, available for the healthcare consumer, facilitating rational

65

decision making regarding health matters. The cumulative effects of such decisions would eventually reduce healthcare costs to their employees, while not compromising the quality of healthcare that the workers receive. The effect would also augment, by reducing the numbers of the poor, the seeming trend for example of decreasing growth of Medicaid spending, which increased by just 2.8% in FY2006, the least increase in a decade[14], state tax revenue simultaneously increasing by 3.7%. Both trends likely indicate that Medicaid is perhaps putting behind it the days of states limiting eligibility, benefits, and reimbursement rates for health-care services in their efforts to reduce costs. In fact, just five states intend to restrict eligibility in 2007, 26 planning to restore benefits, ease application/enrollment limitations, and initiate new outreach efforts.

There is no doubt that Medicaid is growing but its growth is not wild, states taking the initiative to improve health services with the overall economy showing signs of improvement, which underscores the need to embrace measures, such promoting the widespread diffusion of healthcare information and communication technologies, that could further help in this regard. Thus by making it likelier that small firms, which as we noted earlier continue to employ increasing numbers of Americans, fewer would be unemployed, reducing the numbers of the poor, hence the pressure on Medicaid, which would in turn be better able to serve those that need it, hence contributing toward improving the overall health of the nation. Its annual costs are over $300 billion and it caters for over 50 million people, both figures increasing during hard economic periods, more people are out of work and financially challenged, when it is also toughest for states to pay their 40% of overall Medicaid costs, as tax revenues slump. It is also when therefore Medicaid embarks on cost cutting measures with of course adverse consequences for the poor and disabled. Matters improve when the economy does, but should Medicaid have to go through these cyclical changes, when it could prevent them by promoting the implementation of healthcare information and communication technologies, among other measures, and should it not be exploring this option vigorously? Experts argue that the slow growth in Medicaid spending mentioned earlier would even have been slower if it did not have to pay billions of dollars for the new Medicare drug benefit, among whose beneficiaries roughly 6 million low-income individuals that previously obtained prescriptions via Medicaid were. The electronic fiasco that the drug benefit occasioned mentioned earlier indicates the need for both Medicare and Medicaid, and indeed, other healthcare organizations, and providers to embrace healthcare ICT, in particular as with improvements in the economy among other factors result in more enrollment. Such other factors for examples, the increase in the numbers of retirees as baby-boomers retire, population aging, and the increasing population of the country, now 300 million, many immigrants, illegal, and many persons lacking health insurance, would be increasingly important not just for these two organizations, but for the overall U.S health system. Medicaid enrollment increased by 1.6% in FY2006, the least since 1999, and with just 4% of the Medicaid population, typically the elderly and disabled making up 48% of the its 2001 spending, it is not difficult to see what effects these factors would have on its budget in the near future. This underscores the need for it to engage more in intersectoral collaboration as it is for example doing in recent times merging expansion and outreach with a new focus on disease prevention and effective health-care services management. In attempting to control service utilization for example, which is one of its main goals in recent times, should Medicaid not explore the potentials of healthcare ICT in achieving this goal, and would it not need to encourage healthcare providers, to implement these technologies, perhaps even reward them for doing so? Could these technologies then, properly deployed at all levels of say primary, secondary, and tertiary disease not help the organization in achieving its goals, especially with many states planning to broaden coverage in 2007, and the fact that they would have little but no choice to do so when the factors mentioned above become fully operational anyway? California for example has about 95% of Medicaid-eligible children currently enrolled but plans to provide coverage for its uninsured 5%. Such gestures no doubt would involve additional expenditures for the organization, expenditures, which if appropriately utilized would in turn result in less, in the future, with the state having a generally healthier populace. As previously noted, with only roughly 1 in 4 physicians using EHRs in the ambulatory setting, more still needs done in promoting the diffusion of healthcare ICT in the health sector. This important initiative considering the plans mentioned above to increase Medicaid coverage for example, and the factors mentioned earlier would impose broadening coverage in the next few years by these health organizations. This initiative would also involve a focus again, as we have repeatedly emphasized on resolving the CCC, among others for example, convincing doctors and other healthcare professionals that implementing these technologies is ultimately in their best interests, and ensuring the right mix of competition and collaboration to achieve the desired goals. It is unlikely to be too complicated for contemporary healthcare providers to see the wisdom in for example, creating value-added services for its clients that would involve some investments in healthcare ICT but would also help create the distinctiveness the practice might need to gain competitive advantage in the market. By garnering such advantage, patronage would increase, as would likely the bottom-line, which makes collaborating with say Medicaid on implementing these technologies less of threat but rather potentially beneficial. What is more, Medicaid might in fact decide to offer incentives to healthcare providers some way or another to implement the technologies, for example, to physicians that offer/promote primary prevention programs. Consider the increasing use of virtual trainers for examples that come in various forms these days, from audio programs available on Apple Computer's iTunes Web site to

Sony's interactive, humanoid trainers. Doctors acknowledge the benefits of these technologies to the healthcare consumer, but many such as Dr. Aurelia Nattiv, UCLA Sports Medicine physician and professor at the UCLA School of Medicine, cautions could not substitute entirely for a supervised exercise program. According to Nattiv, "Caution should be taken with these programs, especially with the elderly or anyone who has chronic medical conditions or is a novice exerciser". This no doubt, is the sort of advice doctors should give their patients, and which should attract some reward, even if the practice does not have an established gym as some in fact currently do, as part of their overall primary prevention initiatives. Some users could be in danger not being under supervision or receiving feedback regarding if they were doing the exercises the right way. With National Center for Health Statistics data showing that 30% of American adults are obese and 16% of children and teens overweight, getting people to burn off the calories literally is no doubt desirable in achieving the national health goal of cutting down the prevalence of obesity among adults to less than 15% by 2010. Furthermore, with, as noted by the U.S. Centers for Disease Control, the prevalence actually increasing, the need for concerted efforts toward reducing obesity is in fact urgent, and the virtual trainers and other healthcare ICT-based programs could no doubt make a difference. Increasingly used are Nike + iPod Sport Kit for example that measures a user's activity via sensors embedded in the shoes and it wirelessly transmits the data to a receiver in the iPod Nano portable music player, uses music pre-loaded onto the user's iPod to develop appropriate workouts, complete with coaching, inspirational, and training advice. It also links with a Web-based workout calendar thus able to monitor the user's progress. Others such as Sony and Nike Motionworks and Konami's "Dance Dance Revolution", (DDR), the former for example targeted via the firm's virtual video game workout "Kinetic"" at women aged 18 to 34, a group with children already hooked on its PlayStation 2, "Kinetic" workouts led by virtual trainers Matt and Anna, who monitor trainees are also increasingly popular. Besides offering advice to their patients on who should and should not use these technologies, doctors could also oversee the virtual trainers, "virtually" via technological links that alert trainees' doctors to potentially dangerous changes in the trainees' physiology, to accomplish which creates opportunities for vendors to develop appropriate innovative healthcare ICT. Thus we see the complex interplay of a variety of competitive forces that could coalesce in collaboration to result in the achievement of a common objective, everyone or organization involved with the potential to benefit from being involved. In other words, the initiation of efforts say by Medicaid to involve doctors in its goal, albeit with offers of incentives, led to doctors coming up with new ideas on current technologies, which would not only enable more people, including even the elderly and infirm participate in exercise programs. Such participation has the potential to solve a variety of health problems including obesity, dealing with which and its health consequences guzzles substantial healthcare funds, but the doctors' new ideas also create business opportunities for healthcare ICT vendors. Medicaid and indeed, the overall health system also ultimately achieve the dual healthcare delivery goals. Do these scenarios not speak to the need to focus on the CCC at every opportunity in our efforts to achieve these goals? Do they not also underscore the valuable roles of healthcare information and communication technologies in achieving them? The following example also underscores these roles. Not long ago, the U.S Congress set aside a $1 billion fund to reimburse providers for emergency medical services given to illegal immigrants who do not pay their medical bills, but why are these providers not signing up for it? Why is it only 6% of which according to the Chicago Tribune of the funds $12.1 million, for which hospitals doctors, and ambulances could apply in Illinois spent[16]? In fact, not a dime of the funds has gone to Stroger Hospital, Illinois' largest public hospital where 40% of its patients' bills are not paid. Many believe that one reason for this state of affairs is concern about time-consuming paperwork that can offset any money gained, another that questioning patients about immigration status will scare off already petrified immigrants. Could deploying the appropriate healthcare ICT not reduce substantially this paperwork, and could these technologies not also help with immigration documentation that would not identify each particular individual, yet provide a mine of data that the Immigration department or any other government agency would still find useful, data required for policing immigrants obtained someway else? Would these measures not help achieve the original goals for setting up these funds, reducing the financial burden on ER departments, and offering needed services to immigrants, not doing which would only worsen their health problems and swell the ranks of ER visitors even more, so long as illegal immigrants exist in the country? With the costs of unpaid ER bills for illegal immigrants roughly $190 million for hospitals, along the US border with Mexico alone, the Census Bureau recently noting an increase in uninsured Americans to a record 46.6 million in 2005, 15.9% of overall population, and the medical care amount written off soaring, action on healthcare to these groups is rife. Hence, the need to make such measures as the funds mentioned earlier work, which as we noted implementing the right healthcare ICT could help achieve, beside also underlining the importance of blending competition with collaboration that we have so much emphasized thus far in resolving the CCC. As noted Carla Luggiero, senior associate director for federal relations at the American Hospital Association, "There are hospitals that say, 'I am only going to get 33 cents on the dollar and then I have to hire people to complete these forms and house them.' They say it is not worth the effort...On the other hand, something is better than nothing is so we are going to do it. There is a schism there", even hospitals need to and often put their strategic interests in the equation in taking any decisions including receiving free money, with which it could in fact conflict. It is important as part of efforts to resolve the CCC in this instance, as indeed, in any, to understand first the issues involved, including those in direct or indirect collision with the efforts to get the hospitals to collaborate with the Congress' initiative. Some of the program's problems for example include these hospitals having to pay for a patient's stay in hospital after two days, only which the fund covers ER treatment. Government figures for example indicate that Illinois Masonic submitted $1.3 million in payment requests to the federal government but received reimbursements for just $250,000. The American Hospital Association complained that its members just are not keen to employ extra workers in addition to the red-tapism and ethico-moral issues they have problems with mentioned earlier, the return on investment (RIO) inefficient, as Luggiero put it, an important point considering that most of these hospitals operate under tight budgets. There is no doubt about the ethical dilemma of turning patients away at an ER, legal or illegal immigrants. There is equally none though about the hospitals where they seek treatment remaining on the spot, which they probably would not running essentially on a fiscal "empty". This again is the reason why the resolution of the CCC is a key element of solving the healthcare issues that the U.S health system faces. It is evident from our discussion thus far that the CCC emerges on scrutiny of these issues in one guise or another, and that the application of the appropriate healthcare information and communication technologies is crucial in many instances to resolving the conundrums.

The point about resolving the CCC is essentially that we need to accept the

fact that both competition and collaboration exist, and that we need to start to view them differently from before, not as adversary and incompatible, but as bendable characteristics of the healthcare process, and that the outcome of blending them would be maximizing the potentials of both. We cannot discountenance for example that, according to the National Coalition on Health Care, employer health care premiums in the country on the average for a family of four in 2005 was $11,000, which could create conflicts for the needs of the not-so-financially-endowed. On the other hand, could we ignore the fact that in 2004, the country spent 16% of its Gross Domestic Product (GDP) on health, according to the U.S. Department of Commerce, projected to increase to 25% in three decades? Could we also ignore the fact for example that the Medicare Advantage plans, for example also costing taxpayers an extra $2.7 billion in 2005 and $4.6 billion in 2006, which would no doubt put pressure on other domains of the country's economy? Should we therefore not be offering such families opportunities for collaboration, including in particular easing the financial burden of healthcare costs, for example, promoting the use of healthcare ICT, say the virtual exercise programs mentioned earlier that could keep the family healthier and eventually reduce health spending? The launching on October 13, 2006, by the CMS of a revised "Drug Plan Finder" on the Medicare Web site to assist recipients in comparing 2007 Medicare prescription drug plans is another example of such initiatives[17]. This online tool includes cost and coverage information on Medicare drug plans, and several enhancements over the original prototype for example a feature designed to help recipients determine monthly costs, and to create a monthly cost chart for each plan. Besides assisting the elderly to establish when they will enter the coverage fissure, this could help recipients sort plans based on issues they deem most significant, for example the coverage at different times, locations of pharmacies and monthly premiums, obviating potential conflicts with their other commitments. In the 2007 doughnut hole provision for example, would it not help recipients to know that they will pay for 100% of prescription drug costs between $2,400 and $5,451.25, the for 2006 being from $2,250 to $5,100? In soliciting collaboration among seniors for example, would CMS as it did in a release also on October 16, 2006 of an analysis that showed that beneficiaries enrolled in Medicare stand-along prescription drug plans will save on the average 53% versus individuals without prescription drug coverage, not be making resolution of the CCC for some seniors easier? The analysis, which looked at prices for the commonest treatments recipients receive for such medical illnesses as high blood pressure, high cholesterol and heart failure, also showed that recipients enrolled in the lowest-priced plans will in fact save up to 68%, those who in addition use generic drugs, up to 87% off brand-name drug prices. Given these figures, would the employment of for example, targeted, and contextualized health information dissemination to these recipients on drug prices to compliment the online tool mentioned earlier, in particular for those that request it not help them even more in making decisions about these medications? Indeed, the Medicare Rights Center and California Health Advocates for examples recently released a report requesting CMS to require Medicare drug plans to provide "timely and accurate" responses to recipients' queries regarding the drug coverage. Does this not underscore the point about the need for seniors to have as much information as possible, as parts of our efforts to rectify the information asymmetry that could derail these drug programs? Should we also not be implementing the appropriate programs that would help the country's health systems achieve the dual healthcare delivery goals, such as implementing the appropriate healthcare ICT to address whatever CCC we identify within the systems? Consider also the fact that the health sector is a major employer in the country, as in fact is the service sector in general, healthcare having added 1.7 million jobs since 2001. Is it surprising, given the increasing healthcare costs and increasing employment in the health care industry that Alaska has embraced as noted earlier, savings-based or defined-contribution pension plans instead of traditional pension/retiree health plans, for new employees? Why should it be some would contend considering as the Alaska Division of Retirement and Benefits noted that the annual amount the state pays for basic health care more than $10,000 per employee for some retirees[18]? In fact, health care and social assistance made up less than 10% of the state's total non-agricultural workforce in 2002, increasing between 2002 and 2005 by 23% versus 5.3% for the latter. Of the 41% of the growth in non-agricultural workforce, in three years, 6,284 more workers in health care out of a total rise of 15,171, was in the health care and social assistance sector, an undisputable pointer to the accelerating demand for health care in the state. This increasing demand of course, has costs implications, which would make it difficult to contend the state's efforts to pursue the dual healthcare delivery goals, as should any other state in the U.S and the federal government for that matter. Indeed, some attribute the increasing demand and health spending in the state to essentially ineffective restraints on healthcare providers' pricing besides an aging population, and industry direct-to-consumer (DTC) advertising, among other factors, which again calls for understanding the underlying issues with regard each of these and other relevant factors and resolving the CCC so revealed. The approaches of the private sector in Alaska for example to addressing increasing healthcare costs is for an increased interest in buying increasingly high deductible health insurance, not providing any healthcare at all, or tightening workers' eligibility for it, some even cutting down wages increase rates to lessen the total compensations costs. U.S. Department of Labor figures attest to the latter, inflation-adjusted, average pay per hour down by 0.5% in 2001-05, real total compensation, in other words, wages and benefits combined, rising a mere 2.5% during those years. Does this translate to wages pegged due to increasing healthcare costs, and would wages in fact start to fall for the same reasons somewhere down the road as baby-boomers retire, for example? Are these not sufficient reason for us to pursue vigorously the dual healthcare delivery objectives, considering that falling wages would in the health compromise access to health services with the burden of disease at family and societal levels increasing, people even more unable to afford healthcare and the health system catering for even more ill people, costs progressively escalating? These prospects are no doubt real and avoiding them vital. This among other reasons including those mentioned earlier make the need to embrace the CCC model not just urgent but imperative, since by identifying the issues involved in any particular health jurisdiction, we would be able to determine the competition/conflicts and potential areas for collaboration, which would move us ever closer to achieving the dual healthcare delivery goals. Thus, we should again emphasize the need to identify the issues, and indeed, the sub-issues and processes involved, essentially to engage in the decomposition/exposition exercise that would reveal them, a process cycle analysis that would also help us determine the solutions to the problems, including the appropriate healthcare information and communication technologies required as parts of these solutions. The blend of competition and collaboration could be at different levels, and involve different categories of players in the healthcare delivery process. Geisinger Health System and IBM for example plan to collaborate on developing a data-mining project that will draw on information obtained from the former's electronic health record (EHR) system to spot clinical trends and benchmarks with a view to improving treatment outcomes[19]. Noted Brett Davis, IBM Global Solutions Healthcare Executive the pivot of the collaboration, the Clinical Decision Intelligence System (CDIS), open-standard technologies-based, will "drive quality of care, administrative efficiency, and innovation across a number of fronts." The project exemplifies the points we have thus far made about even competition coexisting with collaboration, the best of both emerging thereof as Ronald Paulus, Geisinger's chief health-information technology officer noted, "This is an outgrowth of our commitment to health IT." He added, "Geisinger has had EHRs for 10 years, but we wanted to be able to organize our data in a way that would allow us to gain more clinical insight. We didn't have the resources to develop this internally, but during discussions with IBM we recognized we shared a vision about the need to integrate real-time clinical data with historical data." With CDIS for example capable of use in cardiac risk projection, wherein novel decision support and analytical tools would enable doctors to compare clinical information about a current cardiac patient with the outcomes of previous patients of the same age and health status, the potential of this alliance to improve healthcare delivery is certainly not in doubt. Again noted Davis, "What we're beginning to see is the development and maturation of an analytical environment that can ultimately be used to drive innovation in the healthcare system...Geisinger is trying to create a healthcare analytics system that is a 'closed loop,' which generates quality data and then returns that data to the patient care process." This also underlines the point that healthcare delivery and healthcare ICT essentially are in a symbiosis, with progress in one feeding into the other, creating for example, new approaches to care that would move us progressively closer, in an endless cycle of quality improvement to our health services to as near perfect as they could. It also does the value of process analysis in healthcare delivery and its possible operations at again different levels in the entire healthcare delivery enterprise, and involving different peoples and departments, both within the health field and outside it. Again, noted Paulus, "This will provide us with a treasure trove of analytical information...It will help us determine which patients might qualify for clinical trials and will help drive utilization of evidence-based standards. It will allow us to build on locally-derived best practices, " as we noted above would inspire the development of newer technologies to address some of the new challenges this higher care levels generate, new technologies that would in turn trigger re-conceptualizations of current practice, the cycle continuing ad infinitum. It is clear from the foregoing that we are going to need to start to view healthcare delivery in the U.S from the bottom up, so to say, employing some potent theoretical postulates as the foundation of a veritable health edifice that we plan to build. This edifice would be self-perpetuating with all the relevant concepts in place, to drive it along this path of enduring progress. The U.S health system would likely face increasing pressure as the population ages and baby-boomers retire in 2011. It is time we started thinking seriously about the problems confronting the health system now to avoid them becoming compounded down the road, which since we are unable to find solutions to them now we would be hard-pressed to claim we could and would do so then. There are indications about threat by some in Congress to cut Medicare payments as a means of compelling physicians to agree to tie Medicare payments to government –set quality measures. As we have noted here, we could achieve this clearly desirable goal by blending competition with collaboration, rather than pursuing one to the other's exclusion, this theme, which we have illustrated with different instances and scenarios an important strategic reorientation in our approach to addressing the various issues confronting the U.S. health system. There are many in fact that do not see the need for Congress to essentially micro-manage healthcare, rewarding and evaluating healthcare delivery, market forces best placed to do that. Others have advocated that Congress limit "pay-for-performance" to private Medicare plans, yet others that it promotes increased enrollment in private plans by giving seniors risk-adjusted vouchers as opposed to a specific benefit[20]. Even with market forces involved, competition working in alliance is, as we have argued in this discussion no doubt key to achieving this objective, and indeed, any other in our efforts to achieve the dual healthcare delivery goals.

References

1. Available at: http://www.nj.com/news/ledger/index.ssf?/base/news-9/1160455110190710.xml&coll=1 Accessed on October 10, 2006

2. Available at: http://web.mit.edu/newsoffice/2006/plagues.html Accessed on October 11, 2006

3. McGinnis JM, Foege WH. Actual causes of death in the United States. JAMA. 1993; 270:2207-2212.

4. The White House. Homeland Security -- funding by initiative area. Available at: http://www.whitehouse.gov/homeland/homeland_security_charts.html Accessed October 11, 2006.

5. Hearne SA, Segal LM, Earls MJ, Juliano C, Stephens T. Ready or not? Protecting the public's health from diseases, disasters, and bioterrorism 2005. Trust for America's Health. Available at: http://healthyamericans.org/reports/bioterror05/bioterror05Report.pdf Accessed on October 11, 2006.

6. Levi J, Juliano C, Segal LM, Earls MJ. Shortchanging America's health 2006: a state-by-state look at how federal public health dollars are spent. Trust for America's Health. Available at: http://healthyamericans.org/reports/shortchanging06/ShortchangingReport.pdf Accessed on October 11, 2006.

7. Available at:
http://ec.europa.eu/information_society/newsroom/cf/document.cfm?action=
display&doc_id=176
Accessed on October 12, 2006

8. Available at:
http://www.rwjf.org/files/publications/other/EHRReport0609.pdf
Accessed on October 12, 2006

9. Available at: http://www.kaisernetwork.org.
Accessed on October 13, 2006

10. Available at: http://news.com.com/Europe+extends+open-
source+resource/2100-7344_3-6125383.html Accessed on October 13, 2006

11. Available at: http://www.cato.org/pubs/tbb/tbb_0925-40.pdf Accessed on
October 14, 2006

12. Available at: www.state.nj.us/benefitsreview Accessed on October 14, 2006

13. Available at: http://www.cms.hhs.gov/PrescriptionDrugCovGenIn/
Accessed on October 15, 2006

14. Available at: http://www.washingtonpost.com/wp-
dyn/content/article/2006/10/10/AR2006101001151_pf.html Accessed on
October 15, 2006

15. Available at: http://news.com.com/2102-1046_3-
6125976.html?tag=st.util.print Accessed on October 15, 2006

16. Available at: http://www.chicagotribune.com/business/chi-0609160218sep17,1,2553306.story Accessed on October 15, 2006

17. Available at:

http://www.kaisernetwork.org/daily_reports/rep_index.cfm?DR_ID=40432
Accessed on October 16, 2006

18. Available at: http://www.adn.com/money/story/8307879p-8204048c.html
Accessed on October 16, 2006

19. Available at: http://www.healthcareitnews.com/story.cms?id=5723
Accessed on October 16, 2006

20. Cannon MF& Tanner MD. Healthy Competition: What's Holding Back Health Care and How to Free It. Cato Institute Publication. September 2005

Healthcare Costs in the U.S. Revisited

In an April 2006 survey sponsored by Harvard and the Robert Wood Johnson

Foundation, 43% of Americans mentioned high costs as one of the two most vital health care issues for government to tackle, 34%, lack of insurance and access to healthcare. Just 15% of Americans named Medicare and the drug benefit, which finished way behind in third place as one of the two most significant health care issues, 11%, choosing low-quality care1. Costs concern the average American regarding the family budget, and most think government is spending too little on healthcare. Indeed, Americans consider healthcare fourth among their priorities for government action according to many recent surveys, for example in an Harris Interactive survey in August 2006, just 13% of those polled named healthcare, Medicare excluded, one of the two most important challenges confronting the country, the first national defense, the second, the economy and jobs. Compared to 1993 when health was the second major national issue, after economy and jobs, healthcare does not seem as important as in the past to Americans. However, it is still more important than many other national issues often deemed as very important such as social security, education, the environment, crime, illegal immigration, unemployment, and poverty, hence Americans still care about their health system, and are indeed, dissatisfied with it. Costs no doubt aggravate lack of insurance, and both restrict access to care, which in turn worsens health status, and feeds into the already compromised cost/healthcare access cycle, one we need to break, and fast. This is more so considering the increase in the number of the nonelderly uninsured for which the fall in those of employers offering health insurance, in spite of improvements in the economy, at least in part accounts, in 2005, up by 1.3 million, from 15.6% to 15.9%, or 46.1million persons[2], based on the U.S. Census August 2006 release. The release also show that the number of uninsured children 18 years and less rose for the first time in seven years, and that the improving economy regardless, the proportion of U.S. workers covered by employer-sponsored insurance were 81.2% and 77.4% in 2001 and 2005, respectively, but is this simply a decline or is it a pattern? What's more, 66% of newly uninsured employees during that period were from low-income families. There was also no rise in Medicaid and SCHIP coverage in 2005 to make up for the fall in employer-sponsored healthcare, and the South and West of the country have higher rates of uninsured workers[2,3]. There is no doubt about the need for all Americans to have and maintain access to health insurance, more so the 15% who lack health insurance, the question that lingers on is what needs done to achieve these goals and to arrest among other patterns that of the decline in the number of nonelderly uninsured that commenced in 2000[3]. Should we increase funding for programs aimed at low-income persons, children and small and medium-sized enterprises, change health insurance laws, consider new healthcare delivery models, or should other states initiate programs offering subsidized healthcare take as in Illinois, or universal healthcare as in Massachusetts, or should we not take some definitive action? That employer-sponsored insurance (ESI) declined and the number of uninsured Americans increased between 2000/03, the decline in the economy could reasonably account for at least partially, as it could the increased number of uninsured children since 2005 as Medicaid/SCHIP coverage could not make up for the fall in ESI anymore, as it did in previous years. The explanation for the problems now of the continued fall in ESI and increased number of the uninsured, even if at a slower rate, is a little more complex, although the more rapid growth in premiums versus wages and incomes, is an important factor as would others, for examples population aging and employment dynamics, which could perpetuate these problems. With more people working in the service industries, most employers in which are the small and medium-sized enterprises (SMEs), are we likely to see an increase in ESI, or with many being self-employed, would increasing premiums make coverage acquisition easier? Should we tax these SMEs' less therefore as an incentive to encourage them to provide their workers ESI? Furthermore, what would the likely implications be for the increase in tax revenues measured as the ratio of tax to Gross Domestic Product (GDP), in many of the Organization for Economic Cooperation and Development (OECD) countries, despite deep cuts in tax rates, according to a new OECD[4]? This situation is an indication of the effects of stronger economic growth resulting in increased corporate profits on the one hand, and on the other, some countries' efforts to counterbalance the consequences of tax rates reduction by expanding the tax base and buoying tax compliance. In the U.S. for example, as in Iceland and the U.K., the OECD trio with the largest increase in tax ratio, personal or corporate taxes did not increase, yet income tax revenues, both personal and corporate, have increased. Thus, what are the implications for healthcare access and delivery of a stronger U.S economy resulting in higher tax ratios as firms become more profitable and personal incomes increase, hence the taxes they pay also increase? How could we create the enabling milieu for corporations large and small, to continue to thrive hence be more favorably disposed to providing ESI, therefore improve access to healthcare, and would this require tax cuts, both personal and corporate? The most recent edition of the OECD annual Revenue Statistics publication show that in 2005, tax burdens as a percentage of GDP increased in 17 out of the 24 countries and decreased in only five countries. Table 1 shows total tax revenues as percentage of GDP for the U.S, Canada, the U.K., and Mexico, between 1975 and 2005₄. Besides Iceland, where the tax burden increased 3.7 percentage points to 42.4% of GDP, the U.S had the largest increase, up 1.3 points to 26.8% of GDP, the U.K, up 1.2 points to 37.2%₄. These figures show an apparent reversal of the trend among OECD countries towards lower tax burdens between 2000 and 2003, when the tax ratio decreased from 36.6% to 35.8% of GDP, but increased in 2004 to 35.9%, periods corresponding in the U.S for example, with evidence of decline and improvement in the economy, respectively. Should we aim for a lower tax-to-GDP ratio in the U.S, to increase funds available for healthcare in

	1975	1985	1990	1995	2000	2003	2004	2005 Provisional
Canada	32.0	32.5	35.9	35.6	35.6	33.6	33.5	33.5
Mexico		17.0	17.3	16.7	18.5	19.0	19.0	19.8
United States	25.6	25.6	27.3	27.9	29.9	25.7	25.5	26.8
United Kingdom	35.3	37.7	36.5	35.0	37.2	35.4	36.0	37.2

Table 1: Total tax revenues as percentage of GDP. Source OECD₄

both personal and corporate hands? As in Iceland, where an extra factor was more revenue from taxes on goods and services, should we explore a balance between revenue generation in these versus personal and corporate taxes, with more of the former for example than the latter? There is no doubt that we need to address these and other pertinent questions on the demand side of the healthcare delivery equation, one that would make more funds available to meet the demands for healthcare delivery. Social security contributions also play a key role in revenue generation in many countries, besides taxes on personal income and corporate profits, the significance of these different tax sources for the U.S., Canada, and the U.K., shown in Figure 1. Which of these sources should we

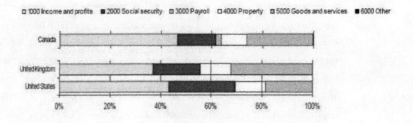

Figure 1: Chart revenues of main headings as percentage of total tax revenues in 2004. Source: OECD4

cut and which should we increase to achieve our goal of increasing funds that are available for healthcare delivery? In New Zealand, most of the country's revenues derive from taxes on income and profits, social security contributions, the main source for the Czech Republic, and taxes on goods and services, for Mexico. The consequences for the health systems in different countries of the sources of revenue generation and for healthcare delivery would be different depending on several factors in particular, the country's funding model of its health system. In other words, it depends on if it had a publicly funded health system, one that private funds operate, or a combination of both, or any other funding model for that matter. This brings to the fore, the importance of the supply side of healthcare delivery, the costs of health services provision to governments, state and federal, in the U.S., and the potential or otherwise of these governments to spend more on these services, for example, as the American public thinks they should. On the other hand, is not the public albeit indirectly seeking what it perceives as the optimal quality of its health services? In short, is the American public not simply interested in health services that work, in having unfettered access to affordable, high quality healthcare delivery? Would it really matter to the American public if governments in the country spent more or less on healthcare delivery so long as it meets its expectations? It is clear from the previously mentioned that we need to explore avenues to meeting the expectations of the American public of its health services from both the demand and supply ends. Both ends, it is equally clear, have significant implications for healthcare costs, which in turn have implications for access to healthcare and the provision of qualitative health services. Thus, we need reduce healthcare costs, for practical reasons, to say the least regarding the demand side, if we wanted more Americans to access healthcare. However, we also need to, and could reduce costs on the supply side to broaden the scale and scope of healthcare delivery, which sounds paradoxical, yet is not, hence improve access to care, and to add to the seeming absurdity of this statement, to improve the quality of healthcare delivery. In fact, by achieving these latter goals, what we would call the dual healthcare delivery objectives (DHDO), we would be achieving our demand-side objectives as well, ultimately. What we should really be asking ourselves is how we could achieve the DHDO, but before we explore the options we have, we need to appreciate the potential consequences of not doing so on not just the country's health systems, but in fact on its entire economy. In other words, we need to start to re-conceptualize health as costs-as-investment (CAI) and not just as costs. This is part of a whole approach to rethinking not just costs but the health system in general, costs for example being inevitable we want to minimize in investments yet to maximize their returns. Thus, besides its possibility, that is just being there, it makes more sense to endeavor to reap maximum returns from minimal investment, considering the other needs for which resources might be lacking or in fact non-existent, were we to discountenance basic yet sound economic principles in our investments, including on health services delivery. Therefore, in seeing health as CAI, we accept the fact that we must spend money on health services provision and access, in other words, from both the demand and supply perspectives, but we also want to spend the least amount of money to access/provide the highest

87

quality care, in other words to achieve the dual healthcare delivery objectives. Thus, operators at both the supply and demand ends of healthcare delivery have a stake in achieving the DHDO. Sometimes, the interests of both coincide, sometimes, not, but essentially they need to collaborate to achieve the DHDO, which incidentally is their common goal.

In a recent progress report on OECD governments' efforts over the past year to

improve economic growth, the countries appear to be more adept at introducing reforms to raise labor productivity than at helping increase the number of working individualss. Should the U.S for example be increasing labor productivity, introducing legislation to lessen limitations on business activity and increase competition while doing little or nothing to introduce reforms to encourage people to stay longer at work, for examples removing tax/other incentives for early retirement, or lessening employment protection that hinder job creation? What are the potential effects of these measures on sickness and disability benefits, and of the latter on pensions benefits, and of this in turn on the availability of funds for healthcare delivery, hence access to health services? Should the U.S. not embrace the concept of merging competition with collaboration as opposed to both being mutually exclusive to derive maximum benefits from either? Reinforcing competition among healthcare providers for example, including removing obstacles to foreign direct investments in health services provision, would no doubt bring out the best in them. These providers would be operating based on the dictates of market forces close to or at the levels, if indeed not past them, of the expectations of the increasingly suave healthcare consumer. This would in fact make it possible for governments, which would be able to observe developments from the sidelines, focus on other key policy issues as market forces, in tandem with established institutional mechanisms, for example, the professional bodies that regulate medical practice, and healthcare delivery and related issues, take charge of the main events. Such events include for examples, credentialing and licensing acquisition/maintenance, which would ensure that qualified and untainted professionals are those in the business of delivering healthcare in the first place. The healthcare consumer would then be free to choose which provider to patronize based to start with on this certification, and on other competitive factors related to it, for examples, surgical success rates, and the sophistication of the practice's value propositions, including the use of cutting-edge healthcare information and communication technologies (ICT.) The healthcare consumer for example would also, to access and benefit from these services be equipped even if minimally, with the required healthcare ICT, for example, personal health records (PHR) technologies, or even just a webcam to communicate "in person" virtually with their healthcare providers as necessary. Here we see competition likely compelling healthcare providers to offer distinctive services to garner competitive edge, including deploying appropriate healthcare ICT, the healthcare consumer, following suit, creating opportunities to access the increasingly sophisticated services that healthcare providers offer, the market's competitive forces bringing out the best in these and potentially other healthcare stakeholders. These forces would also likely temper prices, increasing the affordability of services, hence their accessibility, whose cumulative effects would be clearly the achievement of the DHDO. Yet, the country could not afford to ignore the other variables that are crucial to the achievement of these goals, and indeed, its economic growth in the long term. In other words, it needs to introduce policies aimed at raising labor productivity, including promoting competition as with the example above. Nonetheless, with the country recently crossing the 300 million-population mark, does it not also need a viable workforce, that is to endeavor to increase the number of persons working in the country? Does this not mean introducing policy measures to encourage more persons to work, and to remain longer at work, and employers to employ more persons, and to keep them longer? Would essentially marrying these initiatives, which we would call the collaboration initiatives, with the competitive ones, not be the appropriate approach to deriving maximum benefits from both? Here again, we see the need to synchronize the supply, or competitive, end, with the demand, or collaborative end, as near perfect as possible, both ends in fact intertwined competition and collaboration possibly coexisting in either the supply or demand end. By adopting this approach, we would also be setting in motion multidimensional mechanisms for boosting innovation, a key engine of long-term economic growth. Innovation in the healthcare delivery domain for example, would stimulate research interests in the healthcare ICT required to implement/improve it and to address the various novel issues and processes it spawned. These technologies themselves would be the loci for other new ideas in healthcare delivery, in keeping with the increasingly sophisticated expectations of the healthcare consumer, and changing diseases patterns, among others. In other words, the healthcare delivery and health ICT domains would continually feed into each other, with continuing improvements in each other, and in the overall healthcare delivery process. With these improvements would be decreasing transactions costs, with cumulative decrease in healthcare costs at both the supply and demand ends. With institutional arrangements emerging during the dyadic of the supply and demand ends, the information asymmetry that pervades the health industry, with not just the healthcare consumer, but also health insurers, and government agencies not having all the information that they need to complete the transactions in which they engage successfully, attenuated. Again, the attenuation by the deployment of the appropriate healthcare ICT for example, further lessens transaction costs, which constitute major portions of the GNP in developed countries, not least those generated in the profoundly information intensive and complex health sector. This again, emphasizes the need to strengthen rather than hinder the established institutions in the country whose operations largely would help reduce these transaction costs, by for examples offering appropriate incentives and monitoring/penalizing agents, for example doctors, but which would be ineffective tinkered with, the trust reposed in it by stakeholders, for examples principals such as patients, eroded. These issues, we are going to have to deal with contextually as what obtains in Maine, might be different from that in Florida, for example. Thus we encounter the competition-collaboration conundrum (CCC) at different levels and in different flavors even at jurisdictional levels, the roles and commitments of agents vis-à-vis principals changing for a variety of reasons, and the application of institutional versus government regulatory interventions also depending in the main on factors peculiar to each state, albeit within a countrywide structure. It might be easier for government to regulate certain aspects of the transactions and for professional bodies, others, in one state, and the reverse for similar transactions in another, although the goal is for government to extricate itself from such roles as much as possible. Were access to information on professionals the issue, for example, we would take measures such as implementing the appropriate healthcare ICT to make such access easier for responsible professional councils. Market forces for example would then create inherent mechanisms for the healthcare consumer to choose providers based on trusted certification, or to express opinions via hospital/community committees, indirectly entrenching accountability among providers. This is in addition to what the professional council does to ensure it. Accountability further strengthens market operations, ensuring qualitative service delivery, at affordable costs, including the employment of sophisticated healthcare ICT in the delivery of these services, which as noted earlier would stimulate innovation in healthcare delivery, both feeding into each other in a continuum of progress in healthcare delivery and the achievement of the DHDO. We need to be flexible in our approach to healthcare costs, as this would enable us understand the various issues involved in our particular healthcare jurisdictions to adjust them as deemed necessary to achieve the dual healthcare delivery goals. There is no doubt that certain actions need taken at different levels to address healthcare costs issues successfully, and as we have noted thus face, the dimensions of these different levels vary in scale and scope in different health jurisdictions even within the same state. Nonetheless, the federal government is responsible for certain aspects of healthcare delivery, for example Medicare, and in alliance with states, for example, Medicaid. Some of its policies on the economy among others also have potential effects on the health systems. Thus, the need for collaboration between the federal and state governments and between both and the various other players in the healthcare delivery process is also not in doubt. These different healthcare delivery tiers and players however, need to embrace the idea of viewing healthcare costs in essentially new ways, the flexibility of their approach to healthcare enabling the reinventing of the health systems that they operate in accordance with the inevitable changes the system would inherently undergo, and those the dyadic of healthcare delivery and ICT would impose. The ability to adapt to these changes is the key to the continuing progress in healthcare delivery that results in the achievement of the dual healthcare delivery objectives that are so crucial to the healthcare consumer and the health systems alike.

T he example of Switzerland's health system, which has been able to achieve

the key objectives of good health outcomes and universal health coverage, but at a high financial cost, illustrates the need to take the issue of costs seriously and to pursue with vigor, the DHDO. In a new report on the Swiss health system, the OECD and the WHO commended the system's quality but also recommended measures to control its high spending, which underscores the point made earlier about aiming to achieve the DHDO6. The Swiss healthcare system offers universal health-insurance coverage, with access to a variety of modern health services, patient satisfaction, in the main high. However,, the country's health spending as a share of Gross Domestic Product (GDP) is second only to that of the U.S. among OECD countries, yet the health systems of other OECD countries perform just as well, some even better, at lesser cost. In 2003, Switzerland spent 11.5% of Gross Domestic Product (GDP) on health versus the 8.8% OECD average. It spent 11.6% of its GDP on health in 2004 the U.S spent 15.3% that same year, Germany, 10.9%, and France, 10.5%[7]. Healthcare costs have been on the rise in Switzerland, up by 2.4% of GDP between 1990 and 2004, versus the OECD average increase of 1.5%, indicative of the munificent supply and the soaring prices of the services given. This situation could result in the expenditure of increasing proportions of the country's GDP on health, which no doubt would eventually be unsustainable. This is more so with concerns of continuing rise in health spending due to the country's ageing populations, and the implementation of new and by the way expensive healthcare technologies. "Switzerland will have to develop more cost-effective policies if it wants to better control health expenditure in the future," noted John Martin, OECD Director of the Employment, Labor, and Social Affairs Directorate, counsel that no doubt applies to other countries, including the U.S. The health spending per capita between 1999 and 2004 of the U.S., for example, increased in real terms by 5.9% per year on average, which exceeded the OECD average of 5.2% per year[7]. Another aspect of tackling the healthcare costs problem involves examining where exactly the goes, to what use the health system puts, on what the healthcare consumer spends it, for examples keeping in mind our supply and demand side equation of the healthcare process, and of course the interrelatedness of the two. With regard Switzerland, for example, although its overall health expenditures are high, it spends only 2.2% of its health spending on disease prevention and health promotion versus the 2.7% OECD average. As the WHO's Regional Director for Europe, Dr. Marc Danzon noted, "Investing in prevention and health promotion programs would help Swiss health authorities focus on important public health issues such as tobacco and alcohol consumption and on areas in need of more attention such as mental health and obesity. This would promote health and prevent disease in the whole population, by actively targeting people at high risk". There is no doubt about the applicability of this suggestion to the U.S health system, in particular considering the substantial amounts the country spends on pharmaceuticals for example, the country the top spender in 2004, with 752 USD per capita, France next. This is even more significant considering that in the previous decade, the percentage of health expenditure spent on pharmaceuticals in the U.S increased from 8.5% of total health spending in 1994 to 12.3% in 2004, still less than the OECD average of 17.7%. It is also important that in spite of the country's high level of health expenditure it had fewer physicians per capita than in most other OECD countries, 2.4 practicing physicians per 1000 population in 2004, less than the OECD average of 3.0. It had 7.9 nurses per 1000 population in 2002, slightly less than the 8.3 OECD average. It also had fewer acute care beds in 2004, 2.8 per 1000 population versus the OECD average of 4.1 beds per 1000 population. Its number of hospital beds per capita has also fallen, as in fact those of most OECD countries, have, over the past quarter century, from 4.4 beds per 1000 population in 1980 to 2.8 in 2004, in line with a fall in average length of hospital stays and a rise in day-surgery patients. Are these not in fact reasons for the country to pay even more attention to disease prevention, and in fact the tripartite primary, secondary, and tertiary disease prevention models, in combination for example with an emphasis on ambulatory/domiciliary care? Would these measures not make healthcare more readily available to the many retiring seniors and persons with disability that have difficulty going to the hospital or clinics to seek healthcare? Are such services not in fact, better suited and more cost-effective for the management of the chronic diseases that many seniors have and are in fact becoming increasingly prevalent and constitute veritable healthcare-funds guzzlers? Would such service "re-engineering" not in fact create innovative service offerings at all prevention levels, for examples, the use of a variety of healthcare information and communication technologies that would improve the efficiency and cost-effectiveness of service delivery? Would these measures not eventually facilitate the achievement of the dual healthcare delivery objectives? The OECD/WHO report mentioned above indeed recommended measures to increase the cost-effectiveness of the health system in Switzerland, for example, new reimbursement methods for care delivered, arguing that the method presently used, to pay both doctors and hospitals, namely fee-for service or by number of bed days, have not stimulated strong incentives to increase cost efficiency. This is another key subject in rethinking healthcare costs issues in the U.S., the report recommending for Switzerland for example, a payment approach based on fixed prices per pathology for inpatient care, for example, which it noted would increase service provision efficiency and result in shorter hospital stays. It also recommended increased reliance on gatekeeper/family doctors and less on fee-for-service payment models in primary care. No doubt, the peculiarities of the Swiss and American health systems would determine which reimbursement approaches best suit each jurisdiction. However, in a situation, where as noted above the number of healthcare providers is not optimal, nor for that matter, their distribution across the country the subject of healthcare provider reimbursement is crucial to the provision of qualitative health services to Americans, including the adoption of differential remuneration approaches. Each healthcare jurisdiction, for example, at state levels might also need to adopt recruitment and retention approaches including the establishment of incentives, based on the needs of the particular jurisdictions. We also need to acknowledge the important roles that the widespread diffusion of healthcare ICT could play in ameliorating these provider shortage problems, and in enabling the achievement of the DHDO. That physicians and other healthcare providers are central to healthcare delivery is not in doubt, hence also is that investing in recruiting and retaining these professionals would ultimately contribute to improving healthcare delivery and with less morbidities and mortalities consequent upon this, also to reducing healthcare costs overall. This is why each health jurisdiction should be able to offer incentives it deems fit and could afford, albeit within certain countrywide standards, to attract professionals, and why the provision of providers and of services with public funds should strive to be effective and efficiency simultaneously to attract and retain healthcare professionals. This is also, why it makes sense to offer incentives, for example, funds to these healthcare professionals, to encourage them adopt healthcare ICT that would help in the accomplishment of the variety of health initiatives capable of moving the health system toward achieving the DHDO. The point is that with 45% of health spending in the U.S funded by government revenue, even if way below the OECD average of 73%, the stakes could not be higher that government has in seeing to it that the health system works, and that it is not only for those with the financial wherewithal. The OECD/WHO report also recommended for example that the Swiss authorities in controlling costs through competitive markets should restrict the prospects of insurers selecting insurees based on their health risk, but that they should rather contract with providers based on quality. It also suggested that individuals purchasing health insurance should seek the best coverage at the least premium. Do these recommendations not underscore ours of the need to pursue the DHDO at both the supply and demand ends of the healthcare delivery process? Do the suggestions in the report of enhanced competition in the market for nonpatented drugs for examples generics, helping to reduce prices for pharmaceuticals, and that competition in both insurance and health services provision should cross canton boundaries, not underline the need to encourage optimal market forces operations to improve service quality and moderate service prices? In Switzerland, despite that, insurance premium financing is regressive and out-of-pocket payments, high, versus most other OECD countries, the current premium subsidies and cost-sharing exemptions ensure that susceptible groups could also access quality healthcare. Nonetheless, large cross-canton differences in subsidy levels and eligibility conditions exist, the report recommending the establishment of minimum national standards, the idea of minimum standards which again, as we noted earlier, applies to the U.S., to ensure that the freedom that states and health jurisdictions have do not create excessive disparities in healthcare delivery standards in the country. The idea in fact is that such standards would ensure there is none, the inter-jurisdictional differences that might exist in health services delivery, not critical to the delivery of standard, evidence-based services across the country. The OECD/WHO recommendations on Switzerland also included changes in health-system governance, including the need to develop consistent national policies competitive markets for health insurance, healthcare services and for medications. The report also stressed the need for an all-inclusive legal scaffold for health that would encompass current laws on health insurance, future policies on prevention, national health data collection/collation, and health-system performance oversight. The report envisaged this scaffold would specify national goals and funding responsibilities and ensure the widespread access to health insurance and supply. The varieties of health and non-health related issues on which this report touch, many applicable to the U.S. health system, albeit with the appropriate modifications based on local flavors, indicate the complexity of the healthcare delivery process and the need for a detailed exploration of these issues in any efforts to improve the process.

S uch explorations would reveal the most appropriate solutions to the

problems the U.S health system confronts in particular health jurisdictions and in general. They would reveal the potential for merging competition and collaboration, for example, and for bringing out the best of both to the benefit of the health system in question. On October 19, 2006, Wal-Mart Stores announced plans to expand a generic prescription-drug discount program that the company introduced in Florida in September 2006, to 14 more statess. The program, under which some company pharmacies would offer 30-day prescriptions of some generic medications for $4, would at first, include 65 Wal-Mart, Sam's Club, and Neighborhood Market pharmacies in the Tampa, Fla., area, expanding statewide in early 2007 and to other states down the road. Wal-Mart plans to expand the program to Alaska, Arizona, Arkansas, Delaware, Illinois, Indiana, Nevada, New Jersey, New Mexico, New York, North Carolina, Oregon, Texas, and Vermont, although regulatory and legal requirements in some states could potentially cause delays. This is no doubt a gesture by a potential competitor at collaboration toward the achievement of the DHDO, and which attests to the possibility of competition working in tandem with collaboration, and which we should encourage as part of our efforts at reducing healthcare costs in the U.S., without compromising healthcare delivery quality. Generic medications no doubt are typically equally effective as brand name ones, although often much less expensive, the gesture even offering these medications cheaper. Target officials, in response to the gesture, offered to match the prices for generic medications offered by Wal-Mart pharmacies in all of the 14 states minus Alaska and Vermont, where Target has no stores, although other competitors such as Walgreen has no such plans. Even if Wal-Mart made the gesture in reaction to the increasing patronage of Walgreen by seniors, as the latter claims, it is testimony to the operations of market forces moderating prices mentioned earlier, which overall is positive for the achievement of the DHDO. Kmart on its part maintained that company pharmacies since have offered 90-day prescriptions of 184 generic medications for $15 since May 2006, and will continue to offer those prices. As Ken Johnson, senior vice president of the Pharmaceutical Research and Manufacturers of America, noted, "We believe Wal-Mart's new initiative, which provides mostly older, generic drugs at low cost, is one way to improve access to some medicines for some people." Many are critical of the Wal-Mart initiative, some calling it a marketing gimmick, but the point is that we need to encourage competition, which this gesture is a part of, if we were keen to reduce healthcare costs. The country in fact needs to have a competition policy for the health and related sectors that would ensure the protection of competition, and not competitors, pursuant to which has emerged the concept of "competition on the merits" to articulate differentiating conduct that harms competition from those that promote it. Thus we could promote "competition on the merits," meaning that a dominant enterprise could lawfully engage in conduct within the ambit of the phrase, regardless that the conduct could potentially force competitors out of the market, or hinder their entry into it, although we need to strictly define the perimeter of the ambit, and the underlying principles that defines it. However, it is not likely to be easy defining clear principles and values that represent excellent competition policy. Worse still, we need to decide on competitive practices that government would regulate via legislation and those best left to relevant institutions, or even "consumer exit". No doubt, as part of our efforts to reduce healthcare costs and in fact to achieve the DHDO, the need to revisit competition laws is rife as it is necessary to delineate and expunge harmful, exclusionary conduct while we encourage and retain healthy, competitive ones. As we noted earlier with the Wal-Mart gesture, it is important to acknowledge its competitiveness and the benefits it would have for patients and for healthcare delivery in the country. However, it is also important to ensure it is not harmful conduct to competition in general, since this is what we are more interested in fostering rather than any company in particular. It is necessary to emphasize this point considering the role we expect competition to play in the overall healthcare delivery process that would lead to the achievement of the dual healthcare delivery objectives. Hence, we should consider applying specific tests for detecting harmful conduct such as the profit sacrifice test, the no economic sense test, the equally efficient firm test, and any of various consumer welfare balancing tests, or their modifications as necessary to competition even in the health industry. There is no doubt that none of these tests by itself is foolproof, or suited to every case, or in every jurisdiction. The profit sacrifice test that says conduct is illegal that involves a profit sacrifice, which would be irrational were the conduct not to have a tendency to abolish or lessen competition, for example, could be invaluable in detecting predatory pricing conduct, but deficient in many other instances. It could be over-inclusive, for example, capturing behaviors capable of saving lives although they also bar competitors, such as high R&D costs for a new medication being only rational if the drug's effectiveness were so high competitors remain excluded for the firm to have competitive edge. Thus, we would want to promote such investment and not another for example, where the conduct might entail no short run profit forfeiture, but is harmful to competition. We should be equally eschew under-exclusion, which utilizing the no economic sense test that states that we should not condemn conduct unless it would make no economic sense other than to exclude or reduce competition, would enable us to do as the test does not require profit sacrifice. Furthermore, we could use this test offensively to preempt exclusionary conduct that makes no economic sense, and defensively to accommodate conduct that does, although this does not mean that the test could help us in every case, as it does not for the other tests mentioned above. For example applying consumer welfare balancing objectively and consistently is sometimes challenging, as it is not always straightforward to determine whether conduct enhances or reduces consumer welfare, or to measure the extent of the changes due to the conduct. Additionally, it might be difficult to determine the proper time horizon for applying this test, a choice crucial for dynamic strategies for example, predatory pricing. Also crucial to our application of policies on abusive competition is transparency, ensuring that all concerned are aware of the reasoning behind the decisions made regarding abusive conduct or otherwise, ensuring which could in fact result in healthy discussions that could lead to refinements of the relevant policies and laws. The US Federal Trade Commission actually attempts to explain its no-action decisions even now, which is the appropriate thing to do, which would help with the overall governance of the process of monitoring competition, and ultimately, with regard the health sector, help achieve the DHDO. Competition is an integral aspect of the economy of the U.S., and we need to encourage it in the health sector as well, in ways that the health system eventually benefits. The corollary is also true, hence the need to strengthen the institutional mechanisms for the application of the tests mentioned above, and others that we might deem relevant to particular jurisdictional circumstances, to curb abusive competitive conduct. The relevant regulations and laws should apply to all the players in the healthcare delivery process, health plans, healthcare providers, and others, for examples, to ensure that the activities of any one of these players do not compromise those of others in the quest to ensure the delivery of qualitative health services cost-effectively and efficiently. It is also important to recognize the dyadic of competition and collaboration as mentioned earlier and the need to foster the interplay of both rather than one to the exclusion of the other, which could jeopardize the potential benefits accruable from the interplay. Thus, we need to promote collaboration even among competing interests wherever at all possible. The interplay of competitive and collaborative factors however, may also be quite complex, as for example, the implications of the recent report that HCA Inc., the largest U.S. hospital company posted on October 20, 2006, of a lower third-quarter profit, the cost of treating the increasing numbers of patients lacking health insurance and falling patient volume the key culprits9. There is no doubt that this less than optimal performance would adversely affect the company's finances, hence might compromise its service offerings in particular to the populations mentioned above, and perhaps even in general, considering its stated primary goal being to provide the communities it serves a comprehensive range of quality health care services as cost-effectively as possible. This is more considering its likelihood of strategic and tactical reorientation as it soon metamorphoses in a $21 billion management-inspired leveraged buyout (LBO). Experts believe that this is the largest in history, adjusted for inflation. The company's earnings fell to $240 million or 58 cents per share, from $280 million or 62 cents per share, in 2005. Additionally, could the experience of this company be a marker of trends in the entire industry, in particular regarding patient volume considering the fall in outpatient surgeries? Are the company's problems indicative therefore, of problems that are more entrenched in the health system whose solutions require collaborative efforts between different agencies, including some nonhealth related? With doubtful accounts, or "bad debt," including discounts for the uninsured, increasing to 14.7% of revenue from 13.7% in 2005, could collaborative efforts to prevent such problems for example with the intervention of relevant government agencies, have prevented the company being as it were overwhelmed by the increasing toll of outstanding bills? Could such collaboration for example by Medicare and Medicaid have prevented the flight to its imminent realities by a company that provided healthcare services to the uninsured, were we to arrest the increasing numbers of persons without health insurance, before it bogged down this and several other such firms? Could their "loss," potentially be that of those of the 46 million persons lacking medical insurance, in their care? For HCA for example, uninsured discounts in the third quarters of 2006 were $277 million, in 2005, $241 million, the company's uninsured discount policy, effective in the first quarter of 2005, decreasing revenues and the provision for doubtful accounts correspondingly, in general10. Charity care was $329 million in the third quarter of 2006, versus $298 million in that of 2005. Same facility uninsured admissions, including charity patients, rose by 2,257 admissions or 10.1 percent, in the third quarter of 2006 versus the same period of 2005. These issues might sound at first somewhat obscure, but it is impossible to ignore the fact that the peoples that benefit from them exist and require health services, and indeed, often receive these services, at the expense of the public, or through charity. This is besides the fact that there are about 12 million illegal immigrants in America, who also in the main lack health insurance and receive healthcare some way or another at the public's expense. The need for intersectoral collaboration is therefore crucial in addressing these issues, which constitute a significant drain on public funds, and are major drivers of the country's soaring healthcare costs. Indeed, considering that the country cannot afford to ignore the health of so many of its residents on purely moral grounds, doing so could have catastrophic health and economic consequences. It is therefore crucial to maintain the services portals for the uninsured while simultaneously working on enabling as many of them to have health insurance as possible, and many are out there that could in fact afford to be but choose not to. It is important therefore to establish the mechanisms to ensure the survival of such portals by facilitating their profitability, in a sense their competitiveness at the same time collaborating with them to ensure their survival, for example by ensuring that they do not cave in literally under the yoke of excruciating bad debts. With the increasing competitiveness of the health industry, even hospitals and facilities either publicly funded, owed by the private sector, or by not-for profit foundations, would increasingly need to justify their very survival, let alone expect to thrive. It is going to take the appropriate mix of competition and collaboration to ensure that the cumulative effects of the activities in the players in the health sector work in favor of the achievement by the health system of the dual healthcare delivery objectives.

A s noted earlier, the rising costs of healthcare are of concern at various levels,

the personal, corporate, and the health system levels. Yet, there are underlying issues we need to address to bring everyone on board literally in a concerted effort to address hence, no doubt, eventually solve the healthcare challenges, costs and others, the nation faces. A recent Kaiser Family Foundation poll, for example, conducted in October 2006 showed that nearly half (46%) of voters indicated they were "very worried" about having to pay more for their health care or insurance11. Indeed, healthcare costs woes were at the top of voters' personal worries, fear of their income possibly not keeping pace with rising prices (43%), next. The poll showed that healthcare worries far surpass those about not being able to pay their rent or mortgage, 27%, or the victim of a violent crime, 20%, as they are regarding concerns about losing their jobs, 22%, or being the victim of a terrorist attack, 20%, concern over healthcare costs actually increasing, among women, the chief drivers. Women were likelier than men were to be "very worried" about increasing healthcare costs, 51% to 40%, and to consider health care their most important voting issue, 19% to 10%. Even with Iraq being the most significant election issue nationwide, for twice as many, 30% as any other issue, that healthcare, 15%, was among the next three most significant issues, the economy, 15%, and terrorism, 13%, next in that order, further signifies the importance of the issue. However, that 60% of voters in the above poll indicated that they would vote mainly on the candidates personal characteristics, 37%, or their general sense of what is going on in the country, 24%, versus 35%, about a third, who noted that they would based mainly on issues, is instructive. As KFF President and CEO Drew E. Altman, Ph.D., observed, "It's not enough for the public to worry about health care. Health care needs to compete with other issues, and national candidates need to start talking about health for health reform to break through as a national political and policy priority. " There is no doubt regarding the validity of this concern with a third of voters, 34% indicating that no health care issue was critical to their vote in 2006. According to the poll, regarding specific healthcare issues, voters cited health care costs, 20%, and the number of Americans without health insurance, 18% as the most significant health issue to their vote, just 10% citing Medicare or the new Medicare drug benefit as their most crucial health care issue. However, seniors were likelier to mention Medicare as their key healthcare issue, 22%, versus 8% of young voters. These results are similar to those of the April 2006 Harvard and the Robert Wood Johnson Foundation-sponsored polls mentioned earlier. These polls essentially suggest that healthcare issues are important to Americans, and in particular, the costs of healthcare and the lack of health insurance/accessibility to care, but much need done to heighten awareness of these and other health issues among the American public. These efforts are critical aspects of our overall efforts at not just controlling healthcare costs but also providing qualitative health services. There is no doubt that people would feel the effects on their income of increasing healthcare costs, but would they really know the full ramifications of this increase in their health spending, for example, on their health and those of their families, for example, not being able to afford even basic healthcare? Would they bother about the overall effects of such increases on the health of other families experiencing similar increases, and the potential cumulative effects of these developments on society's overall health, for example, the potential for the rapid spread of diseases that were hitherto almost non-existent, such as Tuberculosis? Would they realize the likelihood of these developments further impoverishing them as their productivity falls, and they are unable to provide for themselves and their families? What about the potential social consequences of these situations, with increase in criminal behavior or even spontaneous riots erupting agitated youths and others unable to contain their frustrations any longer, and would this not further complicate an already bad situation? Could these developments not adversely affect the economy of their states and indeed, of the entire country in the end, witness what is going on in Michigan right now with the high levels of unemployment that the problems the auto-manufacturers face, significantly related to rising healthcare costs to a large extent among the main causes? Should we therefore not increase peoples' awareness of the significance of healthcare issues, and the need for everyone to contribute to solving these problems? This is another example of the sort of rethinking that we need to do regarding not only in our efforts to solve the problems of healthcare costs facing the country, but in fact, those of healthcare at large. Thus, we need this re-conceptualizing at the different levels mentioned earlier and others depending on the approaches we prefer to use in addressing the issues confronting our particular healthcare jurisdiction, and in fact the entire country. We could address the issues at each level also from different perspectives, highlighting the scenarios mentioned above for example, and others at the personal/individual level, and at the corporate level, use a different approach, for example, the emphasis being on competition and collaboration. At the personal/individual level for example, we might want to stress the need for prevention to reduce healthcare costs overall, which would involve emphasizing the need for the public to embrace healthcare information and communication technologies for example that would facilitate the implementation of disease prevention programs. Part of such persuasive efforts would be changing attitudes to these technologies including reassuring the public for example of the safety and security of their personal health information. This in turn of course would require taking transparent institutional measures, for example establishing regulations, and encouraging the stipulation of and compliance with technical standards to ensure that such assurances are not just empty promises. By promoting disease prevention and healthy living in these and many other ways appropriate to our particular health jurisdiction, we would be reducing the costs of healthcare, including those of health insurance. Indeed, with the latter, the 2006 health-confidence survey released on October 25, 2006, by the nonprofit Employee Benefit Research Institute (EBRI) in Washington, D.C., showed that less than 20% of Americans felt satisfied, as they were not with the costs insurance does not cover, over 50% "not too satisfied" or "not at all satisfied[12]". Hence, 60% rated the country's health system as "fair" or "poor". According to Paul Fronstin, director of health research at EBRI and co-author of the study, "There's no change in satisfaction with the quality of care...It is the cost that is driving dissatisfaction with the whole system." This simply underscores the importance of costs to the consumer, as indeed to all healthcare stakeholders. Even as recent studies indicated a decline in soaring healthcare costs, the KKF reporting in September 2006 that increase in health insurance premiums were least in 2006, since 1999, as Fronstin rightly observed, "the 7.7 percent increase is still double the rate of increase of workers' earnings and double the rate of inflation." With health insurance costs for the average family, and individual about $11,500 and $4,200/year, respectively, they are not cheap, and paying more for health insurance, and for health costs insurance do not cover translates to less saving. In fact, over 36% of respondents in the EBRI survey indicating that they had to cut contributions to their retirement savings plans, versus 26% in 2005, 53%, to other savings accounts, versus 45% in 2005, and 28% admitted to problems covering basic expenses, versus 24% in 2005. Would these difficulties not themselves create stress and could the mental health problems that could result, potentially, from these not create physical health problems, and would the combination not result in further increases in healthcare costs, both at the individual, system, and other levels? Do these possible adverse scenarios not also underline the need for us to take healthcare costs issues seriously and seek the solutions to them in our health jurisdictions? Do these issues not in fact have potential social and economic consequences that make tackling them headlong even more urgent? The study also showed that Americans are modifying their behavior regarding healthy lifestyle and healthcare utilization, keener to purchase cheaper but equally effective, generic medications, taking better care of themselves, and speaking with their physicians more carefully about treatment options, and most workers seem to value more firm-sponsored health plans. These observations, all likely related to a better appreciation of the need to reduce healthcare costs, which informs the increasing acceptance of consumer-directed healthcare (CDHC), model, for example, in the country. In fact, another recent study noted that this model, now offered by many employers helps save costs, although might result in some patients skipping some types of care13. The Rand study published in the journal Health Affairs on October 24, 2006, reviewed several others to reveal a composite of the early experience with CDHC, which 3 million to 6 million people now, use, and constitutes about 3% of the commercial insurance market. CDHC demand is rapidly increasing among care purchasers, and as earlier forecasted, it is showing favorable health selection, and resulting lower healthcare costs and lower cost rises. Its consequences for quality are less certain, with evidence of both proper and improper changes in healthcare utilization, as noted earlier, which suggest the need for us to encourage more pricing information provision, for example, to facilitate the most appropriate decision making by the healthcare consumer on provider and treatment options, hence choices. Unlike customary plans where the healthcare consumer would likely pay just about $15-$20 deductible/co-payments for doctor's visits to the doctor, the yearly deductible in a CDHC is typically about $1,050 to $2,000 and $2,100 to $4,000 for individuals, and for families, respectively, the average $220 deductible in a conventional employer-sponsored health plan nowhere near it. As noted earlier, these are expensive for many, even with premiums being lower, or coupling CDHC with health savings accounts (HSAs), which Congress established in 2003, which encourages healthcare consumers to save towards healthcare, and which funds unlike flexible spending accounts, a similar program if unused the consumer could roll over to the next year. CDH is becoming increasing popular, and many companies are planning to offer the plan, nonetheless, no doubt for the reasons confirmed in the Rand study, cost savings, among others, most employers, according to the study, saving up to 10% on healthcare costs, some up to 25%, although some of the costs savings might have ended up passed to the employees. Furthermore, individuals in CDHC seem to be reducing their healthcare spending, 4% to 15% reduction for persons without an HSA in their plan, 2% to 7% for those that have it.

Rational healthcare utilization should not translate however, to service avoidance, which latter the result also noted as being partly responsible for individuals' reduced health spending. Service avoidance for costs reason could mean refusing to visit the doctor for a potentially fatal illness just to save healthcare costs, which would not only do the opposite in the long term, but is also antithetical to the moral principles, and to the achievement of the dual healthcare delivery objectives (DHDO) mentioned earlier. There are also concerns by enrollees about not filling prescriptions or receiving recommended follow-up care. Some have also raised concerns about CDHC attracting more of healthy and the wealthy persons than those sicker and less financially endowed in traditional plans, which could result in the latter plans increasing their rates even more rapidly with the numbers of wealthier enrollees left to share the costs in any given year dwindling. These issues need attention as they have the potential to negate the potential gains from the CDHC plan. The study also noted the difficulty that the healthcare consumer has finding good, consistent information regarding the cost and quality of the health services they receive. This is also important an issue to redress, as it touches on the very foundation of the CDHC model, since without such information the consumer is unlikely to make rational decision about healthcare provider or treatment choices. Hence, the consumer might not be able to save money, or receive the best care at even the exorbitant costs at which he/she is receiving healthcare. These issues again highlight the need for broad-based thinking in our efforts to address healthcare costs issues. It is not enough to implement the CDHC model. But we need to monitor the plan and to rectify its faults, for example, the information asymmetry mentioned above, including encouraging the widespread adoption of healthcare ICT by all healthcare stakeholders that could facilitate bi/multidirectional information exchange, and government for example, establishing standard quality evaluation measures, and expunging legal hindrances to pooling data/information from private health insurers. It is also worth considering, based on the results of further monitoring of the CDHC, to institute measures to discourage the sort of differential enrollment for which some express serious concerns and mentioned earlier. Such measures would prevent CDHC being for just the healthy and wealthy, with the potential to cripple traditional health insurance. Here again, establishing minimum standards of care would be one way to ensure that this does not happen. The question then arises, as it did earlier, regarding whether government or an established institution, such as professional councils establishes these minimum standards, and which of them regulates the standards. The answers to these questions would of course depend on the nature of the standards and the need or otherwise to enforce them, and to what extent. In the best-case scenario, established institutions in the best position to do these jobs, government monitoring progress or otherwise in the background, which would give market forces the freedom to operate and to deliver the best results for all, such as not skewing the health insurance markets. In particular, we need to ensure that we prevent such skewing, which as we noted above could worsen the overall of the public, increasing costs on end-of-care and calamitous health issues which indeed, already make up about 85% of healthcare spending annually in the country. Achieving these goals require extensive inter-sectoral collaboration. The recent efforts of the Office of the National Coordinator for Health Information Technology to ensure the discussion of crossover issues and sharing of recommendations between the new State Alliance for e-Health and the federal advisory group, the American Healthcare Information Community, exemplifies such collaborative measures[14] on issues of significance to both the federal and state advisory groups. The State Alliance is a consensus body established to deal with state-level challenges, state licensure and privacy laws, and other state matters to do with electronic health record (EHR) data exchange, and external to the federal government's jurisdiction, which plans to have its main committee operational by late Jan. 2007, with task forces to follow. This collaboration between the Alliance and AHIC would no doubt help in the facilitating progress in healthcare ICT, and in effect, that of efforts toward achieving President Bush's goal of having electronic health records (EHR) for most Americans within a decade, which in turn would facilitate the achievement of the dual healthcare delivery objectives, including reducing the costs of healthcare. This example also illustrates the multidimensional nature of our efforts at achieving the DHDO, efforts that also involve different domains and organizations many, non-health related, at least on the surface. The implementation of EHR across board, for example, with not just healthcare providers, but also healthcare consumers, health insurance firms and other stakeholders having multi-level authenticated access to aspects of the over system, say a fully integrated National Health Information Network (NHIN) is crucial. Such a system would facilitate the sort of information access to pricing of hospital procedures, healthcare provider profiles, and hospital facility quality, we mentioned earlier crucial to the healthcare consumer taking informed decision regarding his/her health issues, decisions that would ensure access to qualitative healthcare, cost-effectively. Such a network, accessible to private health insurers at different authentication levels for example could, by providing current and accurate, even real time vital health statistics, and other relevant information also help rectify the information asymmetry that also hinders appropriate decision making on premium pricing for example by the health insurance industry. Thus, collaboration is essential across the healthcare stakeholder spectrum were we to achieve the DHDO, and healthcare ICT as we have seen could play a key role in not just achieving this collaboration, but also in helping the various initiatives that could help achieve the DHDO materialize and be efficient and effective. These roles are also multi-level, as the technologies could not only help achieve healthcare initiatives mores efficiently at different disease prevention levels for example, they could also help spawn new healthcare delivery initiatives, progress in both healthcare delivery and in healthcare information and communication technologies feeding into each other. The two become a forward-moving dyadic that results in continuous improvement of health services provision, and eventually in the reduction of healthcare costs without compromising the quality of these services. There are indeed, numerous examples of the collaborative efforts mentioned above, another one, the Puget Sound Health Alliance, a collaboration of several healthcare delivery key players such as providers, purchasers, payers, and the health consumer determined to improve the health system. The increasing costs of health coverage for public employees was a major factor in the decision by Washington State's King County Executive to establish the Puget Sound Health Alliance, whose objective is to develop reforms to promote high-quality, evidence-based medicine and procurement with a focus on soaring healthcare costs15. The Alliance leverages its extensive market share to promote improved healthcare delivery value propositions by providers and insurers to consumers. It also encourages healthcare consumers to acquire and indeed provides them the tools and technologies to manage their care more efficiently and effectively, which attests to the point we made earlier about the need for all healthcare stakeholders to embrace healthcare ICT, which research evidence backs as having the potential to help achieve the DHDO, for example. The Puget Sound Health Alliance, a private, nonprofit body, has over 110 member organizations including public and private employers, health plans, providers and hospitals, and consumers, all determined to utilizing value-based procurement and evidence-based practices to curtail escalating health costs including by optimizing service utilization, and to improve the quality of care, in effect to achieve the DHDO. Among its several initiatives, not surprisingly, is to promote the widespread diffusion of healthcare ICT, including EHR and electronic prescribing, and the improvement of health delivery quality in general, all goals that would likely eventually also lead to the reduction in healthcare costs. The

112

Alliance has four committees, namely health information technology, quality improvement, communication, and an incentives work group. It also has a very active consumer advisory group. The evidence-based treatment guidelines for heart disease and diabetes prepared by the quality improvement committee for example and those it is preparing namely guidelines for treatment of back pain, depression, and pharmaceutical prescribing would form the basis of the sort of minimum treatment standards mentioned above to which every provider ought to adhere in health services delivery. The Alliance plans to publish a report in early 2007, comparing data on quality, cost, and patient experiences in clinics and hospitals regionwide. It is also using measures contained in the Institute of Medicine's 2005 *Performance Measurement* report, and currently compiling insurance claims data for analysis[16]. The Alliance also has a one-page "toolkits" for healthcare consumers. This kit contains the steps that they need to follow to work effectively with providers in disease prevention and management, and plan to develop other kits that employers and union/consumer representatives would use, and to make recommendations on ways by which they could support their employees' healthy living. Furthermore, the incentives work group is developing proposals for aligning incentives for employees and providers, taking employee-benefit design and pay-for-performance (P4P) programs into context. It is also encouraging medical clinics and hospitals to adopt policies, for examples not allowing unrestricted access by drug representatives to doctors and restricting the distribution of free drug samples, which reduce or eradicate the effect of drug sales and marketing on healthcare provider prescribing choices.

There is no doubt about the potential value of this Alliance for the achievement of the DHDO, and the need for such collaborative efforts across the U.S. The Alliance quite modestly acknowledge the need to give its initiatives time to mature and for their benefits to become manifest for examples in changes in employee benefit packages or general adoption of evidence-based care guidelines. Nonetheless, it perseveres in its mission, its members in full support. King County, for example is developing a health assessment program for county employees expected to curtail its healthcare cost increases by as much as 30% in the next two years via improved disease diagnosis and management, an initiative of interest to some private employers. While the Alliance might still await evidence for benefits of its initiatives, this does not mean that evidence for the benefits of such collaborative efforts is lacking. For example, the results of a recent study involving a systematic review of all full economic evaluations such as cost-effectiveness and cost-utility analyses, on enhancement strategies proposed to improve the quality and outcome of care for depression in primary care settings showed that the interventions based upon collaborative care/case management led to improved outcomes, although had costs implications[17]. There is also evidence that the collaborative spirit is spreading among key power brokers in the country, whose governors, in testimony to the increasing importance of the role of ICT in health care are in full support of a novel broad initiative aimed at making e-health records (EHR) part of everyday life. The National Governors Association (NGA) and the Health and Human Services Department's Office of the National Coordinator for Health IT announced in mid-October 2006, that they were establishing the State Alliance for e-Health initiative[17]. The initiative allows governors, elected officials and other policymakers to collaborate on seeking interstate- and intrastate-based health ICT policies and practices, and provides state officials the chance to discuss solutions to programmatic and legal challenges confronting health information exchange. The NGA intends to involve other associations catering for state interests in the future of the alliance, expected to be a consensus-based, state-level advisory and coordinating body. The alliance would offer states a platform for identifying, evaluating, and delineating ways to resolve state-level issues, for example, the interoperability of electronic health information exchanges. State would also operate via the alliance to improve collaboration and enhance the efficiency and effectiveness of healthcare information and communication technologies, and to solve privacy and security issues on the utilization and sharing of electronic health information, among others. State officials would also be able to learn via the alliance about federal-level initiatives, and to leverage federal resources in developing an interoperable health information exchange. Thus, the potential benefits of collaboration are indeed, immense, hence the need to encourage it at all levels of the health system as part of our efforts to reduce healthcare costs and indeed, to facilitate the achievement of the dual healthcare delivery goals. The country has instituted a number of policy changes to facilitate a transition toward CDHC. For example in laws enacted in 2003 that opened the door for tax-free health savings accounts (HSAs), established as part of the Medicare Prescription Drug, Improvement, and Modernization Act (MMA) of 2003, for coupling with high-deductible insurance policies, in an effort to heighten consumers' cost-sensitivity without exposing them to the financial risk of a catastrophic illness[19]. Proposals by President Bush to make premiums tax-deductible for persons buying HSA plans to boost the nongroup market for CDHC and to expand coverage. There have also been calls to make all health spending tax deductible, to reduce inducement to choose conventional employer-provided health insurance with liberal up-front coverage, and others to apply CDHC concepts to Medicare and Medicaid recipients with chronic illnesses[20]. Health Management Organizations (HMOs) and Preferred Provider Organizations (PPOs) would sooner than later start to feel the pinch, literally of the fast growing CDHC. Nonetheless, even with the healthcare delivery model gaining currency, its success would depend on a variety of factors including that of the collaborative efforts of the many players involved in its operations. Besides the success of a healthcare delivery model, is also that of the health system as a whole, which would require our ability to tap the strengths of each of the delivery models, discarding or modifying their weaknesses. We would need to subject component parts of the health system in our particular jurisdiction and at different other levels to an in-depth decomposition/exposition exercise, which would revel the significant issues and sub-issues relevant to our inquiry. We would in turn, subject these issues and sub-issues to more rigorous analyses, to reveal the most appropriate solutions. They would also reveal the healthcare information and communication technologies we would need to deploy to facilitate/modify the issues/processes for us to accomplish the improvement in the entire health system we need to achieve the dual healthcare delivery goals. This exercise, the process cycle analysis, constitutes the underlying initiative that we need to conduct in addressing any of the issues we consider germane to reducing healthcare costs and in fact to achieving the DHDO. It would enable the broad-minded and flexible approach to solving these problems that we so far advocated. This is because by not having a full grasp of the issues confronting our health system, whatever solution we devise could only result in partial success. There is also no doubt about the complexity of these issues, and the need for a variety of approaches to solving them, which with process cycle analyses we would have in surfeit, as each analysis does not have to come up with the same solution, a meta-analysis sometimes likely how we would tease out the best approach to adopt. At the end of the day, we would have arrived at the best comprehensive solution to the problems we set out to solve, and would be able to offer our health system the best in moving it forward. Indeed, as we would need to conduct this exercise on a regular basis, as part of our continuous quality improvement initiative, we could in effect guarantee enduring high quality healthcare delivery, and by extension, delivering the services efficiently and cost-effectively, thereby achieving the dual healthcare delivery objectives on an equally lasting basis.

References

1. Available at:

http://content.healthaffairs.org/cgi/content/abstract/hlthaff.25.w508 Accessed on October 20, 2006

2. Available at: http://www.kff.org/uninsured/upload/7571.pdf Accessed on October 21, 2006

3. U.S. Census Bureau, "Income, Poverty, and Health Insurance Coverage in the United States: 2005" August 2006.

4. Available at:

http://www.oecd.org/documentprint/0,2744,en_2649_201185_37504715_1_1_1_1,00.html Accessed on October 21, 2006

5. Available at:

http://www.oecd.org/document/21/0,2340,en_2649_201185_36060373_1_1_1_1,00.html Accessed on October 21, 2006

6. Available at:

http://www.oecd.org/documentprint/0,2744,en_2649_201185_37562223_1_1_1_1,00.html Accessed on October 22, 2006

7. Available at: http://www.oecd.org/dataoecd/29/52/36960035.pdf Accessed on October 22, 2006

8. Available at:

http://www.kaisernetwork.org/daily_reports/rep_index.cfm?DR_ID=40571 Accessed on October 22, 2006

9. Available at: http://www.medscape.com/viewarticle/546367 Accessed on October 22, 2006

10. Available at: http://phx.corporate-ir.net/phoenix.zhtml?c=63489&p=irol-newsArticle&ID=919064&highlight= Accessed on October 23, 2006

11. Available at: http://www.kff.org/kaiserpolls/pomr102306pkg.cfm Accessed on October 23, 2006

12. Available at: http://www.azstarnet.com/allheadlines/152617.php Accessed on October 25, 2006

13. *Health Affairs* 25 (2006): w516-w530 (published online 24 October 2006; 10.1377/ hlthaff.25.w516) Available at:

http://content.healthaffairs.org/cgi/content/abstract/hlthaff.25.w516 Accessed on October 25, 2006

14. Available at: http://www.healthcareitnews.com/story.cms?id=5761 Accessed on October 25, 2006

15. Available at: www.pugetsoundhealthAlliance.org Accessed on October 25, 2006

16. Institute of Medicine, Performance Measurement: Accelerating Improvement, Washington, D.C.: National Academies Press, December 2005.

17. Gilbody S, Bower P, and Chitty P. Costs and consequences of enhanced primary care for depression: Systematic review of randomized economic evaluations Br J Psychiatry 2006; 189:297-308

18. Available at:

http://www.washingtontechnology.com/news/1_1/daily_news/29573-1.html
Accessed on October 25, 2006

19. Available at:

http://content.healthaffairs.org/cgi/reprint/hlthaff.25.w516v1.pdf Accessed on
October 25, 2006

20. J. Frogue, "The Future of Medicaid: Consumer-directed Care," Backgrounder
no. 1618 (Washington: Heritage Foundation, 2003).

Does America Need Another Health Sector Reform?

Several characteristics of the American health system seem to create inequities

in access to health services and in service provision resulting in urban/rural and rich/poor variations for examples, even along ethnic lines. A study published on October 25, 2006 in the *Journal of the American Medical Association* notes that black Medicare beneficiaries "fare worse" than white beneficiaries regardless of being on the same health plan. Harvard and Brown Universities researchers who reviewed the medical status of over 430,000 Medicare beneficiaries enrolled in 151 health plans between 2002 and 2004 and used four "outcome measures "for diabetes, hypertension and heart disease. The researchers found the most prominent disparity in health in individuals with heart diseases among whom, 72% and 57% of white and black participants, respectively, had their cholesterol levels well controlled. The study concludes that racial health care disparities are not attributable to high- or low-performing health plans or to regional variations and notes that the problem is widespread and deeply rooted in a variety of medical, social, and economic factors. Physician/healthcare consumer information asymmetry, and lifestyle/dietary habit differences, are no doubt among these factors, the need to determine all of which, to be able to find solutions to the underlying problem is not just important but also critical and urgent in the interest of the survival of the country's overall health system. Even without considering the racial and other disparities, their potential to worsen the health of individuals creating additional pressure on the already overstretched healthcare pecuniary resource bases of the country, and on the health system in many other ways as a result, is clear. So then, do we need to reform health plans? That most health plans could significantly improve their outcomes not just for blacks, but for all racial groups is not in doubt, after all there is no reason why only 72% of whites should have their cholesterol levels under control either. The point is that we need to address not just racial or other kinds of disparities in the health system, but also in fact seek to improve the quality healthcare delivery in general, and to do so simultaneously controlling the country's seemingly ever-increasing health spending. Another study published in the same issue of *JAMA* shows that racial minorities are considerably less likely than whites are to undergo major surgeries at high-volume hospitals with proven expertise in the procedures, such as heart bypass surgery, lung cancer surgery and knee replacement surgery, black patients less likely than do white patients to undergo six of the surgeries[1]. The study also shows that Asian patients were less likely than white patients to undergo five of the surgeries were and that the Latino patient was less likely than the white patient was to undergo nine. Additionally, the study reveals that Medicare recipients were more likely than Medicaid beneficiaries were to undergo the surgeries at high-volume hospitals, these disparities still present even after the researchers adjusted the study's results for income, age, and patients' nearness to high-volume hospitals. However, minorities lacking knowledge of hospital quality may be an important factor to consider among others, which underscores the need to address the information asymmetry problems mentioned in any effort at health reform. A recent study published in October 2006 in the journal *Cancer* shows the survival rates of black women who had breast cancer to be lower than did those of white and Latino women with the same condition[2]. The study also indicates that black patients had more advanced cancer when they commenced treatment. Could the breast cancer tumors be more destructive/less treatment responsive in black women since all the women in the study received the same treatment? No doubt, these are dimensions warranting further research but the fact remains that tackling the disparities in the country's health system and improving access to health services require urgent attention. Currents efforts such as those of the National Cancer Institute over the past ten years in tackling the health and other issues pertaining to the underprivileged and medically underserved, racial/ethnic minorities, and rural residents, in particular via the Special Populations Networks (SPN) program are commendable[3, 4]. The Special Populations Networks (SPN) program between 2000 and 2005 actively initiated programs aimed at reducing cancer disparities by promoting cancer awareness and creating chances for community-based research efforts. So are laudable certain recent developments, for example America's Health Insurance Plans announced on October 25, 2006 that it would announce a plan in November 2006 to provide health care coverage to all uninsured U.S. residents[5], a plan that would involve private sector and government collaboration at national and state levels, with a focus on disease prevention and early intervention. Another significant development is Wal-Mart's announcement on October 26, 2006 announced that it plans to expand a generic prescription-drug discount program it introduced in September 2006, to 12 other states[6]. The program, wherein some company pharmacies would sell 30-day prescriptions of certain generic drugs for $4, initially included, 65 Wal-Mart, Sam's Club and Neighborhood Market pharmacies in the Tampa, Fla., expanded statewide in early October 2006. Plans are now afoot to expand it, according to the latest notice, to Alabama, Georgia, Iowa, Kansas, Maryland, Michigan, Mississippi, Missouri, New Hampshire, Ohio, South Dakota, and Virginia, thence to even more states in the near future. Other companies are following suit.

Target plans to match the prices for generic medications Wal-Mart pharmacies offer, Walgreen and CVS officials noted that company pharmacies already offer the same generic medications in the Wal-Mart program for $5 or less, and BJ's Wholesale Club's, that company pharmacies will sell 30-day prescriptions of some generic medications for $4. On October 25, 2006, Giant Eagle and Meijer also announced programs wherein they will offer customers at some company pharmacies generic versions of seven antibiotics gratis, the Giant Eagle program even generic versions of four cold medications also free of charges, and customers qualify their health insurance status notwithstanding. As Meijer President Mark Murray noted, Wal-Mart has raised the generic medications prices issue "to a new level for all retailers". In a related development, the Pennsylvania House on October 26, 2006 voted 176-19 to approve a consensus bill aimed at expanding the eligibility for the state's SCHIP program to many more children7. Children of families with yearly incomes of up to 300% of the federal poverty level, about $60,000 for a family of four are eligible for coverage under the bill the family however, would need to pay part of the premium. Also eligible, are children of families meeting specific criteria, for examples that have health problems excluding them from private insurance and annual incomes above 300% of the poverty level, but would have to pay the full premium. These developments point to the efforts in various quarters to increase healthcare coverage hence improve access to health services. They underscore what intersectoral collaboration in tackling healthcare delivery issues in the country could achieve, and the need to promote such efforts. Yet, they also highlight the multidimensional nature of the problems confronting the country's health system, which range from disparities in healthcare access, to the increasing costs of healthcare and the large numbers of the uninsured, even to dysfunctional resource availability and service utilization. The developments also highlight the need to confront the challenges the health system faces vigorously and urgently. Consider Medicaid, for example. Some would argue for broadening its scope, others for dismantling it, both advancing their reasons, of course, many of which make intuitive sense. Few would argue that the poor for example should lack access to health services simply by being financially-challenged, yet there is no doubt that Medicaid has its problems, some considered even harmful by its opponents, for example even simply broadening its scope, which some deem would swell enrollment and increase its already excruciating financial burden. Some are not enthused by the program's current more than $1000 and rising per capita burden, its potential to increase dependency on government, and indirectly foster "big government," the program's economic loss of about $70 billion, even about state governments kowtowing to Washington on several Medicaid-related issues including funds' disbursement. Some do not even consider the program's overall health impact consequential. Others advocate block-granting it, which would give states the freehand to reform health services in their jurisdictions more effectively, the idea of leaving Medicaid to the unfettered dictates of market forces enough to make yet others cringe, apprehensive of the fate of the underprivileged given these circumstances. Then again, the question remains whether in fact, America needs another health reform, or a set of health reforms at state, even other levels, or indeed, does it simply need to make the system as currently constituted, work more efficiently and effectively. On the other hand, do we in fact need to reconsider the meaning of health sector reform (HSR), for example backing off the prevalent idea in the HSR zeitgeist, re-conceptualizing it, abandoning the idea that it is a panacea for all the country's healthcare delivery needs? To be sure, HSR has essentially failed in many countries in the past, in Colombia between 1995 and 2005, the gains in increasing equities in access and resource allocation offset by the dramatic rise, over 10% of the country's Gross Domestic Product (GDP), in health spending, which compromised the underprivileged essentially outside the system, benefiting from these gainss. Decentralization of health services administration in Guatemala during the same period, reduced health spending but the resource allocation problems that resulted, further heightened inequities in healthcare access, and the introduction of user fees in self-governing hospitals adversely compromised health services access/utilization by the poor in Honduras and Peru. However, should these examples mean that there is no place for effective and sustainable health reforms? If not, how should we proceed in reforming health services in America, focus first on primary care, for example, or on incremental in tandem multilevel care approaches, and what role, if any, should government play in these reforms? Would we in fact need to reinvent the conceptual basis on which the answers to these questions depend?

There is no doubt about concerns regarding the failure of government in HSR

as the examples in Latin America given above shows, yet some would argue that market forces left unregulated would also be catastrophic for health services, the operations of which left solely determined by competitive forces. Many would favor regulatory government intervention in certain elements of HSR, while others would argue that established institutions should be the regulatory agencies as they would be more effective, perhaps more trusted by the public than government, to whose bureaucratic baggage many attribute the inequities in access to health and many of the flaws in healthcare delivery. The need to shed this baggage, some others would deem the reason for improving government performance, in particular, the management skills of its officials being a key, and perhaps even among the first objectives of any health reform effort in the U.S. This in turn brings to the fore, the perennial issue of who, administrators, or medical professionals, best suits the executive management echelon in the health sector. There are also important issues regarding the approaches to management regardless of who best fits the executive slot, for example, the emphasis or otherwise on hierarchical or horizontal management approaches9. The overcentralized nature of the former, some would contend results in aloof decision-making including budgetary, removed from the realities "on the ground", with a tendency to be inept and ineffectual, and lacking in accountability, none of which bodes well for the delivery of qualitative health services, efficiently and cost-effectively, what we would henceforth term the dual healthcare delivery objectives (DHDO.) To what extent then should we attempt to reform the public sector to achieve our overall healthcare reform goals? Some would argue that the public sector should also be subject to competitive forces, while other would contend that we need to consider the political/institutional milieu in which the public sector operates to under stand why the need for the managerial autonomy for example that is integral to effective participation in the competitive marketplace may not materialize. While it may be true that such lack of autonomy might reflect political pressure to ensure "political correctness" that we would have to start seriously considering exfoliating administrative bureaucracy and improving the effectiveness and efficiency of the public health sector is not in doubt. This is more so, considering the imperative, as this is the effective operational position, of the need to achieve the DHDO, for a variety of reasons. Are the issues mentioned above, which no doubt warrant our attention, important elements of the HSR the American health system needs, therefore, indicative of the answer to our earlier questions regarding the need or otherwise for another HSR in America? With regard the public sector for example, should we as part of this HSR embrace the concept of hospital autonomy or corporatization and to what extent, in other words, should we structure and make our public health facilities operate as private sector organizations do, and to what extent? Should we promote more competition in health services provision, liberalize even more, outsource to, and subsidize private health services providers? Should we as part of the reform efforts reexamine resource allocation/utilization vis-à-vis reimbursement for service provision by healthcare providers at individual and organizational levels, and what criteria for example would we use to couple performance and quality with reward and incentives for examples? Should we and to what extent should we integrate the healthcare consumer in healthcare delivery for example broadening consumer choice latitude and fostering consumer empowerment, and what policy measures should we take to ensure the consumer, whose expectations of the health services incidentally continues to be increasingly sophisticated, actually has the resources required to make such choices? What role would the widespread implementation of healthcare information and communication technologies (ICT) play in the achievement of these goals, and indeed in rectifying the pervasive information asymmetry that plagues the health industry, which certainly, even if not possible to totally eliminate, hampers the achievement of the DHDO? Should our efforts at reforming the country's health sector not also involve ensuring accountability not only on the part of healthcare providers, but in fact, also regarding other players in the healthcare delivery process? Considering the escalating costs of healthcare, should we not be seeking health financing from non-tax revenue sources, for example via some sort of cost-sharing arrangements, user fees, and others deemed useful, and which would not land us in a quagmire exaggerating the problems of access to health and the inequities in healthcare delivery we aim solve? Would our efforts to achieve the DHDO not be consistent with improving the efficiency, effectiveness, quality, equity, and sustainability that would constitute the main objectives of health reforms? Many would not contend the desirability of these noble objectives, nor likely dispute the fact that reform packages are legion, and that they are not typically value-neutral, often colored by local hues of social, political, and other opinions, and often operational in tandem with ongoing reforms in other public sector domains. In other words, should not then be considering instituting the appropriate reforms in other sectors of the economy to make our proposed health sector reforms work, for example, embracing the general principle of government being more involved in policy making, acquisition, and regulation, rather than being involved directly with healthcare provision? In other words, as Osborne and Gaebler (1992) noted, would we need to "reinvent government", as part of our health reform efforts? There is no doubt from the previously mentioned that the country needs health reforms, some of whose elements we have also mentioned. In fact, the country needs theses reforms on an ongoing basis. The health sector is profoundly information-intensive. Additionally the information is fluid, changing in the different sectoral domains, both health and non-health at a fast pace, in particular in the health domain. These changes necessarily impinge on healthcare delivery, sometimes in dramatic ways, as for example, the potential changes that would occur, at all healthcare delivery levels upon the unexpected emergence of a particularly virulent strain of bird flu. We would no doubt need to make far-reaching adjustments to our healthcare delivery operations under such circumstances, bringing the health system to different baseline operational level at least with regard some activities, including the implementation of new healthcare information and communication technologies, for example. This new level and the required structural and functional changes that accompany it would essentially be the template for further progress in healthcare delivery. Thus, for example, progress in the healthcare ICT domain could inspire new healthcare delivery initiatives to address the problems the arrival of our health system at the new level generate, for example to improve certain processes, or modify them, including their exclusion, from the process, the resulting progress in healthcare delivery in turn the trigger for innovative novel technologies. In effect, progress in the healthcare delivery domain feeds into the healthcare ICT domain, resulting in progress in the latter, which in turn feeds into the healthcare delivery domain resulting in progress in that as well. Both domains, therefore, engage in a symbiotic dyadic whose endless cycle of interrelatedness forms the basis of a continuous quality improvement cycle that culminates in the delivery of qualitative health services, and indeed, in the achievement of the DHDO. In other words, the health sector, and indeed, other sectors of the economy is inherently unstable, hence needs continuous evaluation, and quality improvement. Put differently, we have no choice but to reform the American health system on an ongoing basis were we to ensure it continues to meet the dual healthcare delivery objectives. Just as the health system, is inherently in a state of flux is it therefore, imperfect, always. This again buttresses the point regarding the need for continuous improvement not just reactively to the disruptive events that would inevitably occur but also as part of our efforts toward making the health system closer to perfection as possible, a necessary strategic intent in our efforts to achieve the DHDO. Thus, even if there were no external health systems against which we could benchmark our goals for the American or any other health system for that matter we could benchmark it against the DHDO, achieving which would no matter how incrementally would therefore be the key driver in our reform efforts. Even without having to worry about soaring healthcare costs, the increasing suaveness of the contemporary healthcare consumer, population aging, and the imminent retirement of large numbers of baby-boomers, does it not make intuitive sense to deliver qualitative health services more cost-effectively, and in fact, for much less money? The point here is that we need to start seeing healthcare delivery in consonance with the realities of our times. Health is clearly an investment and we do not, in our quest to achieve the DHDO purport otherwise. That it does not matter that we spend over 15% and rising of the country's GDP on health services is no longer tenable, if we could deliver equally qualitative services for much less, how we could do that then the real questions we should be asking ourselves thing about health reforms at all. There is no doubt that there would many different ways we could achieve these objectives, and we need to consider them if we wanted to achieve these objectives, but it is also possible that in the process of identifying these approaches we discover the epigenetic nature of the cascade of factors, issues, and processes that underlie healthcare delivery. We could in fact also discover the fundamental strand that traverse this structure, a revelation that could be the basis of a completely new approach to our conceptualizing healthcare delivery and crucial to us achieving the dual healthcare delivery objectives. The above describes another key issue in our efforts at reforming the health services, therefore, one that essentially involves a continuous decomposition/exposition exercise that reveals the salient issues and processes that need modifying/reforming, and the means to doing so, including the appropriate healthcare information and communication technologies to deploy for example in the process of achieving these goals. Indeed, considering the transactional nature of the healthcare delivery enterprise, and indeed, the high transactional costs characteristic of processes, particularly healthcare delivery, in developed countries, healthcare delivery is not only a conglomeration of transactions, a critical aspect of our health reform efforts would involve seeking ways to make these transactions more efficient and less expensive. This includes via the decomposition/exposition or process cycle analysis mentioned earlier, among others. It is therefore going to be important also, in our efforts at reforming the health system in the U.S., to examine the important roles that healthcare ICT plays in not just improving transactional efficiency, but also in reducing transactional costs.

A RAND Corporation study published in September 2005 in the journal *Health Affairs* showed that the country's healthcare system could save over $81 billion yearly and improve the quality of care if it adopted computerized medical records, on a large scale[11]. According to Richard Hillestad, a RAND senior management scientist who led the two-year study, "Our findings strongly suggest that it is time for the government and others who pay for health care to aggressively promote health information technology." The researchers urged government to speed up efforts to establish common standards for healthcare

ICT as a key measure to promote the widespread adoption of these technologies. In fact, they recommended the provision of financial incentives for example increasing Medicare reimbursements to healthcare providers who adopt healthcare ICT, and grants to institutions that also do, by government to speed up the adoption process, which attests to the urgency they attach to the matter. The researchers attributed these costs savings to the electronic medical records systems being able to reduce redundant care, expedite patient treatment, improve safety, and to sustain good health. Would implementing these recommendations therefore not be an important aspect of our health reform efforts, and indeed, as is instituting the relevant policies and establishing the relevant organizations and advisory, working and other committees to tease out the various technical, legal, social, economic and other issues involved in facilitating this implementation? Here again we see the need to broaden our perception of HSR to optimize the potential opportunities available in achieving the results it aims at, and as the examples mentioned earlier shows, not the exact opposite, if at all. The pervasiveness of the potential roles of healthcare information and communication technologies in our HSR efforts is unique considering the enormity of the transactions involved in the healthcare delivery process, these technologies, far from being mere facilitators of many of these processes, with the potential for constitutive or embedded in the processes. By so doing, they become organic aspects of the healthcare delivery process, engaged in a motorized symbiosis the technologies feeding into the processes, and vice versa, in a continuous improvement process as earlier noted. The point then is that the challenges that the American health system faces are complex requiring a comprehensive solution whose determination and delivery however, necessarily require multidirectional collaboration of decentralized and devolved operations of intersectoral public and private as well as public-private dyadic. With each dyadic addressing the issues germane to it, would the emergence of solutions at basic jurisdictional levels of healthcare delivery coalesce into solutions of increasing importance in the health delivery equation on an increasing scope and scale. Thus, we would address problems of the health system at different dyadic levels, within a decentralized structural milieu, the aggregate of the solutions that emerge however, contributing overall to the achievement of the country's healthcare delivery objectives, the DHDO of course also achieved at various other levels including at that of the most basic health jurisdiction. What we are trying to emphasize here is that the broad goals of healthcare reforms are essentially universal, and some of those we mentioned earlier, for examples improving the quality, efficiency, and effectiveness of and ensuring the accessibility, equitability, and sustainability of healthcare delivery are applicable to the U.S. health system. What we need to do is reconceptualize these issues within the context of their local flavors, right from the most basic jurisdictional level. We need to consider for example the variety of services currently provided and the potential for new initiatives based on the evolution of the dyadic mentioned earlier as opposed to normative typologies variations in whose economic features preclude typology-based health services delivery, invariably, including for reasons of perceived potential or real flaws in free market operations. Furthermore, in approaching service delivery flexibly, we need to make the necessary provisions to obviate potential market flaws, here again, the important roles that healthcare information and communication technologies could play, noteworthy. Promoting the widespread diffusion of healthcare information and communication technologies for example would help with ensuring equitable access to health services for typically- expensive conditions such as cancer, at for examples the different prevention levels, utilizing the tripartite disease prevention paradigm. At the primary prevention level for example, via the provision of current and accurate, perhaps even contextualized and targeted health information on preventing cancers, including engaging in healthy life styles, among others. Such efforts would no doubt help reduce the prevalence of these conditions, as they have no doubt helped with certain forms of cancers such as lung cancers[12], although still the leading cancer killer in the country in both males and females, in the latter overtaking breast cancer in 1987, as the number one cause of mortality from cancer[13]. These are reasons why we should not consider preventing this disease trivial. In fact, among the 2000 National Cancer Institute defined cancer prevention and control goals were the following risk-factor diminution goals, namely to cut the percentage adults that smoke to 15% or less and those of children and youth between 12-18 years that smoke to 3% or less. The Institute considered the achievement of these goals would lead to over 40% reduction in lung cancer related deaths, if the current smoking prevalence then persisted into this century. Alas, however, between 1979 and 2003 lung cancer deaths rose 60%, about 162,460 deaths from lung cancer expected this year (2006) in the U.S[13]. With an estimated 90% of lung cancer cases caused by smoking, radon, asbestos and air pollution other notable causes[14], should we not focus our efforts on reducing smoking rates, which are indeed falling among men but remain static since 1983 among women after many years increasing? With the increasing use and sophistication of healthcare ICT devices including mobile and wireless technologies capable of delivering multimedia content in a variety of formats, to different population groups, do we not have ready tools for such targeted health information delivery as mentioned above? Could such initiatives not constitute the real elements of any health reform, executable at all health jurisdictional levels, the cumulative effects of which would reverberate across the entire health system in qualitative and accessible health services delivered efficiently and cost-effectively? Should we not therefore be creating the enabling milieu for the adoption of these technologies on a widespread basis that would result in the offering of such preventive programs by healthcare providers for example, being standard value proposition to an enlightened healthcare consumer populace seeking to achieve the DHDO on an individual level, and understandably and legitimately so? Would these developments not temper prices in a competitive market obviating the need for government's direct involvement in healthcare delivery for a high-cost disease, such as cancer and is this argument not applicable to secondary and tertiary prevention of this condition? In other words, could the operation of market forces not also establish standard value proposition by healthcare providers for the prompt diagnosis and the immediate treatment of this condition based on defined evidence-based guidelines in the first, the definition by the appropriate institution established to set up such guidelines, market forces determining additional minimum standards of care? With regard tertiary prevention, minimal standards acceptable to the markets for the prompt and adequate treatment of the sequelae of this condition, including rehabilitation programs, also would emerge with time, again, tempering prices, making these services more affordable. Healthcare ICT again could play key roles at these levels, such as the evaluation and monitoring of patient's condition at home reducing the need for frequent and costly hospital visits, among others. Do these approaches not attenuate concerns about accessibility to health services by the underprivileged albeit to a certain extent, the mechanisms for subsidizing costly healthcare for the poor, a key proposal by some for preventing this category of American residents not lacking such health services, important to tease out, or it for ensuring that they do not lack such access? The answers to these questions are part of what should comprise our health reform efforts, as equitable access to health services is an important component of the health-sector reform agenda. Having considered the high-level approaches to these questions, and the important roles that healthcare ICT would play in actualizing our healthcare delivery initiatives at the different levels of prevention, we need to consider additional measures to ensure equitable access to those minimum standards at the different prevention levels, still using the tripartite prevention model to illustrate our health reform efforts. These measures would operate mostly at state and health jurisdictional levels based, among others, on regional variations in the prevalence of say lung cancer, demography, the structural, and functional levels of business activities/private sector operations, the educational levels of the populace, and the nature and extent of available institutions. These are factors crucial to the successful operations of market forces relevant to healthcare delivery, and indeed, to market operations in general, and would determine for example the need or otherwise to subsidize health services provision to the poor, and the nature and extent of such subsidies. It is perhaps because of the localness of the key determinants of market success, among other possible reasons, that some advocate the operations of Medicaid for example in the free market, the federal government, simply block granting it as noted earlier. Thus, each state or jurisdictional level might consider such additional measures as healthcare subsidies interim that have healthcare ICT-backed health-information dissemination programs in place whose goal, among others includes rectifying the pervasive information asymmetry that could hinder the successful operations of the market forces that could potentially temper prices and make health services more affordable even for the poor. Another state with more literate populace might not in fact consider such subsidies a priority, as perhaps with much fewer numbers of the poor and uninsured considers Medicaid adequate, perhaps even broadening eligibility and services scope, a better alternative to achieving the same goals, namely the dual healthcare delivery objectives. Such a state might even consider establishing some form of vertical equity-based programs for example mandating health insurance coverage for such individuals paid for by the state in full or in part based on individual needs, in other words some form of subsidies and liberalism in health system financing. It might adopt this approach to ensure that not only do they receive minimal standards of health services, but to better monitor and manage service utilization and obviate the need for haphazard and perhaps even wasteful use of emergency services, and to work toward these individuals taking charge of their healthcare costs in the future for example when gainfully employed.

There is no doubt about the variety of approaches to ensuring that we meet

the ideals of healthcare delivery in America. It is important though that each
state or health jurisdiction and the federal authorities recognize the importance
of utilizing the characteristics of the health sector positively in achieving the
desired objectives, for example, that the sector is highly information intensive,
this information the elements of the many transactions that occur in the process
of delivering health services. An aspect of reducing transaction costs, which as
we noted earlier for example is the application of the information/knowledge
acquired in the most efficient and cost-effective manner for service delivery. A
doctor that lacks information on the most recent guidelines for the treatment of a
particular disease for example is unlikely to treat that disease the best way
he/she should. This has important implications not only for the prolongation of
the illness and of course of the pain and suffering of the patient, but also for the
overall costs involved in the treatment of that patient even if the defect in
treatment resulted in death. What would be the economic and in fact ethical
sense therefore for the doctor and the hospital in which he/she works to invest
so much money and time on building a library for example, or even on any of the
varieties of knowledge management software available on the market, if this
defect still occurred? What if the doctor spent a lot of precious time searching the
medical journals and periodicals for the required information and he/she did not
apply the knowledge acquired appropriately, with the same result obtained as if
lacking in the knowledge? The point here is that part of our health reform efforts
and by extension, those for achieving the dual healthcare delivery objectives is
managing health information efficiently, including ensuring the proper
application of such information in reducing transactional costs. In other words,
part of our reform efforts should involve ensuring at every level of the healthcare
delivery enterprise, the provision of current and accurate information to

healthcare delivery agents, whoever they are, for examples doctors, lab technicians, nurses, and office and ward clerks, to deliver the tasks on behalf of their principals as efficiently as possible. This means ensuring that these agents spend less time sifting through reams of paper or groping for information on the hospital's networks or even using its knowledge management systems if available, when in fact they either do not know where or how to apply the information, or when, or choose to apply the knowledge discriminately based on personal whims. In short, on the one hand we need to invest in the appropriate healthcare information and communication technologies that would facilitate essentially the ferreting of valuable information from a variety of resource areas and databases, and on the other ensure the most efficient application of this information/knowledge. These measures would not just ensure a handsome return on investment on our efforts, including on the technologies we deployed, but also move us forward toward the achievement of the dual healthcare delivery goals. The point about the appropriate applications of information and knowledge is crucial in relation to the promotion of the widespread diffusion of healthcare ICT that we have talked so much about here. This is because health reform essentially implies changing one or more aspects of what we currently do regarding healthcare delivery, and no doubt and considering the central role of transactions in the healthcare delivery process, healthcare ICT could facilitate them, and make them more cost-effective to conduct. However, it is not enough to invest in and implement these technologies. We need to ensure that they do what they ought to do in the transactional process, lest we derive no benefits or not enough to achieve the DHDO. Our efforts must involve changes to all the agents, players, and components of the health system including as Roberts et al (2004) noted every person that offers public or private health care services, such as doctors, nurses, hospitals/clinics, and pharmacies, among others15. The health system also includes the mechanisms that enable the flow of money that finances the system, including user fees, and the activities of those offering specialized

137

resources to the health system, for examples medical and nursing schools, and the manufacturers of medications, resources and medical teams producers. They also include professionals, many who work in Health, Finance, and Planning Ministries, in public and private insurance and in regulatory institutions, responsible for planning, regulating, and acting as financial go-betweens, who control, finance and influence the healthcare services providers. Components of the health system we need to target also include the activities of agencies and bodies providing preventive health care services for examples immunization, family planning, infectious diseases control, and health education, and they could public or private, local or national, or even international. There might be others in our local healthcare jurisdiction that we consider important components of the health system and would want to target as part of the reform process of a particular issue/activity/or process in the healthcare delivery process in our jurisdiction. Indeed, all healthcare stakeholders are part of the health system, and the scope of involvement in a particular reform effort in our jurisdiction would of course vary with the particular issue at hand and with the peculiarities of the jurisdiction. We need to incorporate the elements under consideration in the particular deliberate attempt to change a particular aspect of the American system, even in nonhealth domains for examples interventions in the financing, payment, regulation, purchasing/supplies, and organization domains. We also need to include them in our consideration of the desired short-term performance results such as efficiency, quality, and access to healthcare and performance goals such as healthcare consumer satisfaction, overall population health status, protection against financial risk, and in general the dual healthcare delivery objectives. It is also important for us to be specific regarding the goals that we set out to achieve, which would no doubt help us streamline our efforts and focus our resources toward the achievement of these goals. We need to be sure for example, regarding our intentions to achieve equity in healthcare delivery, whether we are working toward population health equity or service delivery equity, the former, toward ensuring that all residents have the highest level of physical, psychological, and social well-being their biological limitations allow, the latter. The latter involves working toward ensuring equitable resources, services allocation/utilization, and the delivery of health services based on peoples' needs, and financed based on peoples' capacity to pay for the services. Additionally, equity in health refers to such issues as the morbidity/mortality levels in different population segments, for example, and equity in healthcare delivery, such issues as access to health services, and health services financing, and resource allocation and utilization by different population segments. There is no doubt about the importance of each type of equity and of the need for us to target each of them, but it is just as crucial to know which one of them we focus on at any particular time and regarding particular initiatives, even if the two would typically likely overlap in different ways. It is clear from the foregoing that health reform should be an ongoing exercise in the American and even any other health system. It is also clear that we need to address certain high-level issues that pertain to all components and activities that result in healthcare delivery, such as the issue of knowledge acquisition and proper application mentioned earlier. The important role that healthcare information and communication technologies play in modifying/improving healthcare delivery processes and transactions is also not in doubt, as is not the need to tease out the particular health issues we intend to change as part of our health reform efforts. It is also important for us to engage different individuals and organizations in both the public and private sectors of the economy in addressing salient issues that would lead to the changes in the health system that we plan to achieve. Many such intersectoral collaborative efforts are currently underway, focused on specific problems and issues in the healthcare delivery process for example the Partnership for Prescription Assistance, which links qualified, low-income people with discount prescription drugs, direct from the drug companies, thereby facilitating access to care by these underprivileged Americans, helping to solve the equity problems relating to healthcare delivery. The Partnership for Prescription Assistance organizes the interaction between the country's pharmaceutical firms, doctors and other health care providers, patient advocacy and community groups in a bid to assist qualifying patients lacking prescription coverage obtain needed medications via the appropriate public or private programs, free or almost. The PPA, which provides a single point of access to over 275 PPA programs (public and private), including over 150 programs that drug firms offer, plans to raise awareness of patient assistance programs and boost enrollment of eligible persons, to qualify varied by program, income levels, by state. Thus, part of reforming healthcare is strengthening the collaborative efforts between healthcare stakeholders in different sectors in addressing such issues as access to healthcare. Put differently, access to healthcare, for example, a key short-term performance result in our reform efforts, is achievable via a number of different ways, including resolving the competition/collaboration conundrum in both the private and the public sectors, paving the way for blending competition with collaboration, to derive maximum benefits from both as the example of the PPA shows. From a broader perspective, even if some would contend that such examples distort the market, the benefits from the potential for costs reduction due to the prompt and complete resolution of diseases that they engender far outweighs the potential increase in health spending bearing those costs, such programs lacking, would. Thus by reducing costs, such programs enable the health system reduce health spending that we would otherwise have needed to defray soaring healthcare costs, therefore, these programs help us in not just our reform efforts, specifically in this instance, to improve access to care and eliminate inequity, but also in achieving the dual healthcare delivery objectives. Furthermore, by improving access to care for the underprivileged for example, such "subsidy" programs enable the achievement of a short-term goal crucial to that of long terms performance objectives for the health system, some of the beneficiaries of the programs becoming healthy, gainfully employed and economically productive, with no need anymore for the "subsidies," eliminating a cost area. Thus with no costs to bear, health spending falls, and with high quality health services delivered, we achieve the DHDO, which in turns frees up money for use in other sectors of the economy on the one hand, and increases national wealth and spawns sustainable economic development on the other. From the above, it is clear that the pursuit of these objectives of improving access to healthcare and eliminating inequity in the health system are crucial in our efforts to achieve the DHDO. One of the major changes that we want to make to the country's health system is therefore, to increase access to care, and to qualitative healthcare for that matter.

W e need to consider the obstacles to equitable access to healthcare delivery

perhaps as a starting point in our process cycle analyses of the matter, for example, distance and topography, resource scarcity, and organizational issues such as scheduling defects contributory to hospital wait times, for examples. We need to explore the underlying issues and processes and the appropriate solutions to them in our particular healthcare jurisdictions. Such solutions might include fostering telehealth services, ambulatory/domiciliary care, mobile clinical teams/services, and mobile and wireless healthcare delivery. Modifying/changing costs-related inequity in service allocation/utilization for example, besides the subsidies mentioned earlier, could mean financial decentralization, novel approaches to health provider recruitment/retention, and expanding health insurance coverage in a variety of ways, for example broadening the scope of Medicaid and SCHIP. Equity in quality issues would mean establishing appropriate mechanisms to ensure the delivery of minimum standards of healthcare, and the ensuring the required credentialing/certification to ensure the delivery of these standards of care. It would also mean engaging in ongoing quality appraisals that would reveal areas of healthcare delivery for which improvement is crucial and urgent for examples. This again, underscores the need for process cycle analyses as important aspects of our health reform efforts, and performed at the appropriate level, for example health jurisdictional levels, could be crucial in solving the peculiar problems confronting that health jurisdiction, and on the aggregate contribute to the solution of the problem even at the national level. Thus, the experiences of a particular state in implementing for example, a regional health information organization (RHIO) could be invaluable to other states in implementing theirs, and in the implementation of the national health information networks (NHIN.) This example also illustrates the need for decentralization in the health system, in this case not just to give market forces the opportunities to operate freely, but also for technical reasons, and other reasons for example, the potent of the problems of privacy and confidentiality regarding the exchange of personal patient information in the country. This latter reason in particular informed among others recommendations of the major IT vendors that responded to the request for information (RFI) by the Office for the National Coordinator for Healthcare IT (ONCHIT) in November 2004, termed the Interoperability Consortium (IC), comprising among others, Cisco, Microsoft, Accenture, Computer Science Corporation (CSC), Oracle, Hewlett Packard (HP), Intel, and IBM. This recommendation was for a service-oriented, distributed, and federated, NHIN architecture that uses Web Services to link different components/services. It is decentralized and scales to a national level enabling the progressive deployment of several value-added services down the road. The IC in making its recommendations also considered the localness of healthcare activities and the delivery of health services in the main, acknowledging that the RHIO being the conglomeration of many healthcare providers/organizations that would share a common backbone for health data exchange should be that scalable. A collection of RHIOs would therefore be able to transform into the NHIN all of them interoperable via communication mechanisms for example Web Services. Indeed the RHIO prototype is now operational, in three states, Massachusetts, Indiana and California, able to communicate and exchange clinical data via a number of HL7 v2, utilizing the HL7 2.xml standard, and HL7 v3 over Web Services. All operate different commercial Web Services stacks, for examples Sun/Java in Indiana, and Microsoft in Massachusetts, and open source in California, the cross-platform operations nonetheless, seamless. This example also illustrates the need for collaboration among competing organizations in making the proposed changes work, which in the end, all stakeholders would benefit from. It also illustrates the point made earlier as part of the reform process of establishing the appropriate institutions to conduct different aspects of the healthcare reform process. Thus in this instance, the Healthcare IT Standards Panel (HITSP), a component of American National Standards Institute (ANSI) is responsible for recommendations on the required standards, and the Health Information Security and Privacy Collaboration (HISPC), on developing security and privacy guidelines and solutions. The Certification Commission for Health Information Technology (CCHIT), a component of the Health Information and Management Society (HIMSS) is working on how to certify products and solutions in compliance with HITSP and HISPC recommendations. Here we see the variety of organizations involved in an important aspect of the reform process of the American health system that we have been talking about, which is not, at least on the surface health related although critical to our achievement of many of the health sector reform goals mentioned earlier. For examples, the implementation of these technologies would help improve access to care, and eliminate inequity in health services delivery. Indeed, overall they would help in the achievement of the dual healthcare delivery goals. The example also illustrates the point about adopting a more flexible but coordinated approach to addressing health sector reform issues in contemporary times, considering the shifting healthcare delivery paradigms and the influence of progress in healthcare ICT on these new concepts of care. It also shows how we could achieve specific health reform goals based on the outcome of the interactions between these two, and other domains. It would be difficult if not impossible to know the full ramifications of the activities in which we need to engage to address successfully though, a particular health reform issue without the sort of in-depth systematic process cycle analyses mentioned above. It is the revelation of the underlying issues and processes pertaining to the health reform issue that would trigger the continuous decomposition and exposition mentioned above crucial to an understanding of the solutions, including the healthcare ICT required, for the health reform issue. Such analyses would also reveal the nature and extent of the intersectoral collaboration required to achieve the desired objective, the engagement of these different participants in the tasks important to achieving the reform, as the above example shows. Thus, our efforts to reform the American health system needs to be multidimensional in outlook, each healthcare jurisdiction recognizing its particular health issues that need improving and conducting process cycle analyses to determine the way forward in carrying out the reforms. This forward motion as we have noted would involve cross-sectoral issues and processes but also the participation of disparate individuals and organizations, in many cases. In circumstances where we aim to deliver qualitative health services to the healthcare consumer while simultaneously reducing healthcare costs, we want to ensure that our efforts on the former works effectively for the latter, in other words, reduce the need to spend money costs-related health services. Thus, we need to continue to pursue the means to reduce health spending, or put differently to make Americans healthier and to obviate the need to use health services, in particular expensive health services. We would therefore be seeking ways to improve health via the promotion of healthy lifestyles, via disease prevention, and to reduce the use of costly hospital procedures when not needed, in other words to prevent the misuse and abuse of the health system. We would also seek ways to prevent the costs associated with chronicity of diseases, either by preventing them becoming chronic in the first place by promptly diagnosing and treating them in some cases. In those that progress in that direction, whatever we do, we want to make the necessary treatment and rehabilitation services available to arrest the progression and assure the patient's quality of life. However, these efforts would require an initial investment, in particular in the healthcare information and communication technologies for example that could help us achieve many of these goals more efficiently and cost-effectively. This initial investment would no doubt be worth the while in the long term as we would be able to reduce costs due to illnesses, complications, hospitalizations, and chronic care, emphasizing the potential benefits of not just these technologies but in having a flexible, "out-of-the-box" approach to conceptualizing contemporary health sector reform. By reducing costs via the provision of qualitative multi-level health services, we would be reducing the soaring spending on healthcare delivery in the country, yet achieving the dual healthcare delivery objectives. It is clear therefore, that we should expect make initial investments in service delivery as part of our reform efforts, in particular on healthcare information and communication technologies to reap the benefits of these technologies in facilitating qualitative care provision, hence in reducing costs, and eventually health spending, and helping us achieve therefore, the dual healthcare delivery objectives. While many have blamed the high costs of technologies in part for the country's ever-increasing health spending, although most of these have been on sophisticated medical technologies such as CT scanners and Magnetic resonance Imaging (MRI) technologies, there is no doubt that the initial financial outlay on some of the healthcare ICT are also significant. Nonetheless, we would not benefit from these technologies if we did not implement them, and because we acknowledge their potential to help us achieve many of our reform goals, part of the reform efforts we have been discussing therefore should be promoting the implementation of these technologies by all healthcare stakeholders. This is not just important in achieving equity for example in healthcare delivery, but also in health in general, that is population health, which factors outside the health system for examples context-specific features in social, economic, and environmental, among others influence, and which it influences. Hence, the need for involving these different domains in addressing these interplay of issues, a process that the deployment of relevant healthcare ICT would likely facilitate. Thus it would much easier to address the information asymmetry problems that confront and indeed hinder healthcare delivery if we also targeted closing the education/digital divide that exists even between groups in America, the promotion of the widespread diffusion of information technologies likely to help us in achieving both objectives. This would certainly involve collaboration between health and education authorities for example, an alliance that would pay off for both.

One cannot gainsay the importance of these conceptual and other issues in

approaching efforts to improve any healthcare system in contemporary terms. The solutions to specific issues such as Medicare and Medicaid, health insurance coverage and other salient challenges the American health system faces would flow from such theoretical underpinnings. In other words, it is not that there is any "silver bullet" to solving the country's health system woes. Indeed, an aspect of the rethinking of the health system's issues we are discussing here is that there could never be any. This is not just because of the immense complexity of the transactional processes involved in healthcare delivery, with a variety of players and activities involved, but also because the system is inherently subject to change both from within and without. The challenges that emanate from each change therefore would require new solutions, even a fresh approach, as we now argue, to deal with them in the first place, and the changes are legion. This is why it is necessary to have a theoretical framework from which to approach these changes, for example, the need for process cycle analyses on an ongoing basis to reveal the underlying "schisms" so to say that result from these changes. Thus, we would need to relate these disruptions to the status quo so to say in terms of the tactical and operational issues and processes involved, and the extent of modification, and in what direction they would need to keep the system functional at the very least at optimal levels in the new dispensation. In other words, to achieve continual operations of the health system, we might need to introduce new policies and expunge others, or simply modify the latter. Similarly, certain transactional processes might have to go, for example the use of paper records, replaced by electronic health records systems (EHR.) It might also be necessary to establish policies guiding the utilization of some services different from before, and in the governance of not just the administration of health systems, but also even the healthcare information and communication technologies meant to enhance its efficiency. Consider the issue of quality of healthcare delivery for example. In expanding insurance coverage and attempting to reduce the adverse consequences of out-of-pocket healthcare spending by the poor, we also want to ensure that they do not receive poor quality health services. Simultaneously we want to ensure that the physicians receive the appropriate remuneration and incentives for providing these services, yet also prevent the abuse by either of the services. Thus, we have a variety of issues that we need to address to achieve DHDO, requiring an in-depth understanding of the interplay of factors in each transaction, which process cycle analyses would help us achieve. This analysis would reveal for example, regarding say a fee-for-service patient/doctor encounter, details of the encounter and the services rendered obviating the need for dispute over for example, "defensive medicine" with both the patient and the doctor having access to an electronic record system that documents such details. It would also be easier for example with a pay-for-performance (P4P) encounter to determine which doctors receives what remuneration/incentive for the care of a patient with multiple health problems with the relevant technologies implemented. Our efforts to improve the quality of healthcare delivery and to expand health insurance therefore should involve such considerations. By teasing out the salient underlying issues regarding each of these activities in the healthcare delivery process, we are able to appreciate the issues better and to determine the solutions including those based on the deployment of the appropriate healthcare information and communication technologies required in successfully addressing the issues. As earlier noted, such analyses would also inform the need or otherwise to retain or expunge certain issues and processes. It would then be easier to streamline the healthcare delivery processes ensuring that only those processes survive that contribute positively to the efficient and cost-effective running of the country's health services. In other words, we could need for example in expanding health insurance to consider reviewing the social security/pension funds laws. Whatever we do however, should reflect a through appreciation of the issues involved and the coupling of this understanding with the stated goals of the delivery of qualitative health services efficiently and cost-effectively. In other words, we need to appreciate the effects of achieving these goals on the projected ballooning of retirement benefits accruing to the millions of baby-boomers that would retire in the next few years for example. We would have to examine the potential for reducing the anticipated health spending on health that this imminent retirement would engender. As we noted earlier to see whether the reduction in morbidity in the seniors would obviate the need for such high health spending, or if we should adjust to the fact that they would inevitably continue to use health services heavily. If the former, we should as part of the reform efforts ask how we could make baby-boomers less ill and if the latter, from where we would source the funds to provide them cost-effective and qualitative health services. Either way, besides tweaking social security laws, an important consideration would be the role that healthcare ICT could play in for example, disease prevention, and in ambulatory/domiciliary care, which would no doubt be more cost-effective than repeated hospitalizations and would maintain service quality. The point here is that regardless of the issues pertaining to the U.S health system that we want to address, we are likely to encounter processes related to the issue that require the implementation of healthcare information and communication technologies to facilitate, or more broadly speaking, to modify. It is important therefore for us to appreciate the need to invest in these technologies as part of our health sector reform efforts in the country. As we have established, the question really is not whether America needs another health sector, the country's health system needs reforming on an ongoing basis, as does in fact the health system of any other country. The system is inherently unstable and subject to change, some of which could in fact be cataclysmic and for which we might be ill prepared as the example of the aftermath of Hurricane Katrina shows. In fact, part of the reason for the need to adopt the flexible approach to conceptualizing health sector reform we have discussed here is to be better prepared for such unexpected natural or even manmade disruptions of our health services. There is no doubt about the cushioning of the effects of the Hurricane on health services in Louisiana and adjacent states were a full-fledged health information system in place across board for example. With regard, deriving maximum benefits from these technologies regarding our health system our goal is to promote their adoption by as many of the healthcare stakeholders in the country as possible. Another aspect of our health sector reform efforts should therefore be to establish the modalities for such promotion, among healthcare professionals for example, the use of incentives to encourage investments in these technologies. Here again is where the collaboration of different organizations in disparate domains is important, such incentives coming from both the public and private sectors. Software vendors for example might want to make payments and licensing much easier, even offering versions of their software for use free and later upgrades for sale were the physicians to consider them valuable. Such a move by one software company might in fact be the trigger for later competitive pricing that would help increase the acquisition of these software hence their widespread adoption, the more of the software sold, the more profits the vendors likely to make. Health insurance firms might also want to offer software and other technologies or some sort of incentives to encourage doctors to adopt healthcare ICT, as they would benefit also in the process for example regarding facilitation in billing/payments, and in fewer disputes over healthcare providers' claims. We should also promote the use of the technologies by the healthcare consumer, many of the initiatives we mentioned earlier, for example, efforts to reduce the doctor/patient information asymmetry likely to be much easier to deliver. This is not to mention the potential of the enhanced contact between the healthcare consumer and his/her doctor opening immense consultation, even treatment opportunities. That the American health system is imperfect is not surprising, and it will always be imperfect. This might sound harsh but no health system would ever be perfect, because every health system is essentially unstable. Even if it were, would we want to sit idly and not attempt to improve the health system? In other words, it is not just that the health system would remain unstable, hence imperfect, but we are obliged to ensure that we evaluate the system on an ongoing basis to incorporate new knowledge and technological progress, and advances in other areas such as accounting and in management in the evolution of the health system. This is important for us to get as close as achieving the dual healthcare delivery objectives as possible. The American health system also faces enormous challenges in the years ahead, for example due to population aging, and the influx of immigrants that it makes little intuitive sense not to institute reform measures in anticipation of the likely effects of these phenomena on the country's health system. The reforms that the health system would undergo would likely improve it in many ways, but they would also prepare it for the future, and prevent a precipitous arrival at that time that could be disruptive to not just the health system but also the country's economic system and perhaps even its entire social fabric. The health system that anticipates events with potential adverse impact stands a better chance to survive and to thrive, in particular in the emergent global milieu, where failure to attune a country's health system to potential visitation for example by an unknown virus from abroad and to respond to the aftermath of such visitation appropriately, could spell catastrophe. We need to start to rethink health reform in some of the ways we have discussed here to acquire this anticipatory mode and to employ it effectively in continuous health sector reforms. These reforms would ensure that the American peoples enjoy the benefits of qualitative health services delivery, with significant resources left for other sectors of the economy including in ensuring for the country and its peoples sustainable economic growth and development. This underscores the point we made earlier that we need to acknowledge the necessity of an initial financial outlay in our health sector reform efforts, particularly on the healthcare information and communication technologies crucial to the achievement of our dual healthcare delivery objectives. This investment, however, we would recoup in terms of a healthy and productive populace that would be the driving force of the future of the country's economy. Health is therefore a worthwhile investment, rather than being merely costs.

References

1. Liu, JH, Zingmond, DS, McGory, ML, SooHoo, NF, Ettner, SL, Brook, RH, and Ko, CY. Disparities in the Utilization of High-Volume Hospitals for Complex Surgery *JAMA*. 2006; 296:1973-1980.

2Available at:
http://www.kaisernetwork.org/daily_reports/rep_index.cfm?DR_ID=40658
Accessed on October 26, 2006

3. Clanton, M. The National Cancer Institute's special populations networks for cancer awareness, research, and training (p 1931-1932)
Published Online: 6 Sep 2006
Available at: http://www3.interscience.wiley.com/cgi-bin/jissue/113386997
Accessed on October 26, 2006

4. Freeman, HP, and Vydelingum, NA. The role of the special populations networks program in eliminating cancer health disparities (p 1933-1935)
Published Online: 23 Aug 2006
Available at: http://www3.interscience.wiley.com/cgi-bin/jissue/113386997
Accessed on October 26, 2006

5. Available at:
http://www.kaisernetwork.org/daily_reports/rep_hpolicy.cfm#40688 Accessed on October 26, 2006

6. Available at:
http://www.kaisernetwork.org/daily_reports/rep_hpolicy.cfm#40691
Accessed on October 26, 2006

7. Available at: http://www.post-gazette.com/pg/06298/732748-85.stm
Accessed on October 26, 2006

8. Equity and Health Sector Reform in Latin America and the Caribbean from 1995 to 2005: Approaches and Limitations. Report Commissioned by the International Society for Equity in Health – Chapter of the Americas April 2006

9. Grindle, M. and Hildebrand, M. Building sustainable capacity in the public sector: What can be done? *Public Administration and Development*, 1995, 15441-63.

10. Osborne, D and Gaebler, T (1992) Reinventing government; How the October 28, 2006entrepreneurial spirit is transforming the public sector. Plume Books, New York.

11. Available at: http://www.rand.org/news/press.05/09.14.html Accessed on

12. Horm JW, Kessler LG. Falling rates of lung cancer in men in the United States. *Lancet* 1986; I: 425-6.

13. American Cancer Society. Cancer Facts and Figures, 2006
Available at: http://www.lungusa.org/site/pp.asp?c=dvLUK9O0E&b=669263
Accessed on October 28, 2006

14. Alberg AJ and Samet J. Epidemiology of Lung Cancer. *Chest*. Vol. 123, January 2003.

15. Roberts M, Hsiao W, Berman P, Reich M (2004) *Getting health reform right: A guide to improving performance and equity.* Oxford University Press, New York, USA.

Conclusion

We have attempted to X-ray essentially the American health system to

reveal the mechanisms underlying its immense and complex healthcare delivery processes. There is no doubt that the system needs overhauling but this is not necessarily because it has problems, many of which we have discussed in this e-book. That is not to say that it does not and that we should not seek their causes and the solutions to them. On the other hand, what we have established in this e-book is the need for us to re-conceptualize health sector reform. Among other benefits in so doing, we would be able to appreciate the need for the continuous improvement of the quality of health services delivery in the country. In other words, we have seen in the course of our discussion in this book that health systems are inherently unstable, hence subject to internal and external changes. These changes might be minor, with relatively mild impact on the healthcare delivery process, while others might have profound effects on the system. Regardless of the impact, the point is that some change has occurred that we need to incorporate into the workings of the system, essentially changing or reforming the system or some aspect of it. In this sense therefore, we must maintain our quality improvement efforts in fact seeking all changes including minor ones whose cumulative consequences might be worse than even the major ones, to move our health service toward achieving the dual healthcare delivery objectives we have talked so much about in this book.

In adopting, the necessary measures to enable us achieve the dual healthcare

delivery objectives we would need to invest in the health system. Again, as we have seen in our discussion, we would in fact not achieve the objectives without such investments, for example, in the healthcare information and communication technologies crucial to the efficiency and effectiveness of the varied transactions, both health and nonhealth, that characterize the healthcare delivery process. Thus, and crucially, our objective is not to slash healthcare spending for its own sake, since we would end up spending even more, anyway if the costs of healthcare delivery escalate unabated due to the wherewithal for the efficient and effective delivery of these services being sorely lacking. On the other hand we want the American health system to be as near perfection as possible in which case it would be in fact be able to spend less of healthcare while healthcare costs also progressively fall, which intrinsically mandates the delivery of high quality health services. The core of the motorization of the health system that enables the achievement of this status quo, essentially the healthcare information and communication technologies, would work in a symbiotic dyadic with progress in healthcare delivery to facilitate the achievement of this goal. Indeed, as we have also noted, these technologies would play an increasingly significant role in not just our efforts to reform the country's health system, but also in achieving the dual healthcare delivery objectives, to the achievement of which goals all healthcare stakeholders, indeed need to contribute.